Dedicated to the children, staff and volunteers of the NSPCC

From Acorn To Oak
Memories Of Derry

Edited by Stephen Kelly

Pen and ink drawing by Kevin Copeland, age 13, winner of a design competition run in conjunction with the book launch

First published in May 1998 by
Guildhall Press, 41 Great James Street,
L'Derry, Northern Ireland BT48 7DF
Tel: (01504) 364413
Fax: (01504) 372949

© Guildhall Press/Stephen Kelly 1998

ISBN 0 946451 49 4

Cover design – Tim Webster

Printed by Coleraine Printing Company

Guildhall Press receives support from the Training & Employment Agency under the Action for Community Employment scheme. Special thanks to Manus Martin (T&EA), and Derry City Council's Recreation and Leisure Department for generous Community Services Grant Aid.

All rights reserved. No part of this publication may be reproduced or transmitted in any form or by any means, electronic or mechanical, including photocopy, recording, or any information storage or retrieval system, without permission in writing from the publisher. The book is sold subject to the condition that it shall not, by way of trade or otherwise, be lent, re-sold or otherwise circulated without the publisher's prior consent in any form of binding or cover other than that in which it is published and without a similar condition including this condition being imposed on the subsequent purchaser.

Acknowledgements

I would like to thank all those who have taken the time to recall and record their memories of their formative years, special days and observations on our city and its people. The quality of the submissions have been excellent and together paint a unique and colourful picture of our city.

The Foyle District Fund-raising Committee of the NSPCC have over the last number of years been working tirelessly, on a voluntary basis, to help both fund and draw attention to the work of the Foyle Children's Resource Team. Majella McGee, Eamon Gee, Helena McMenimin, Rosemary Warnock, Thomas Quigley, Esdale Hunter, Carita Kerr, Colm Maguire, Libby McCallum, Noel Murray and Chairman Redmond McFadden have all shown their commitment to children. This has to be commended. This commitment is also visible in their fellow committees in Eglinton and Coleraine. If you have some time to spare, please consider joining or helping them in their fund-raising and awareness efforts.

The Guildhall Press, particularly Adrian Kerr and Joe Mc Allister have provided invaluable advice, help and assistance.

The books cover was provided by local artist Tim Webster. I am sure you will agree that it is both striking in appearance and very suitable for this publication. Another illustration in the book is by 13-year-old Kevin Copeland who was the winner of our design competition. The photographs have been provided by the contributors.

Without the financial assistance of our sponsors, The Londonderry Initiative, Long's Supermarkets and the Foyleside Shopping Centre, this publication would not have been possible. These organisations have supported the NSPCC over many years and their continued support is greatly appreciated.

The staff of the NSPCC Foyle Children's Resource Team have also played their part in making this publication work. My thanks go to Danny O'Neill, Seamus O'Hara, Stella McLaughlin, Cathy Tierney, Teresa McDaid, Ann Simpson, Mary Doherty, Esther Sweeney, Peggy Woods, Jean McAteer, Rosalin McClelland, Alma Ward, Stella McParland, Eileen Vaughan, Deirdre Norby, Ann Devenney and Children's Resources Team Manager Ian Elliott. Particular thanks go to Maeve Twells and Phyllis McLaren who had the thankless task of deciphering handwriting and creating word-processed text for the publishers. Their work has not gone unnoticed as has their support for the Team, fund-raisers and voluntary committees over the last number of years.

I hope you enjoy the book.

Stephen Kelly

Contents

NSPCC Foyle Children's Services	9
Introduction – *Councillor Martin Bradley*	10
Welcome – *Lady Moyra Campbell, CVO*	11
Oh How Times Have Changed – *Samuel Adair*	12
Eccentrics Or What? – *Gerry Anderson*	14
The White Horse Inn – *Colum Arbuckle*	17
"It's Never Too Late To Have A Happy Childhood" – *Roy Arbuckle*	23
Memories of Nellie Ramsey, Gacka Wacka And The Palace – *Jimmy Cadden*	26
The Town I Loved So Well – *Phil Coulter*	28
The Sticks – *Jim Craig*	30
Coming Home – *Peter Cunnah*	33
Memories Of Childhood – *Frank Curran*	37
Childhood Memories – *Dana – Rosemary Scallon*	40
College-Boy – *Seamus Deane*	41
"I Remember, I Remember, The House Where I Was Born" – *Sister Anna Doherty*	46
The Apple Of My Mother's Eye – *Paddy Doherty*	49
Cut Knees And Coca Cola – *Roma Downey*	51
Earhart's Aeroplane And The Children's League Of Pity – *James Eaton*	52

In Sunshine Or In Shadow – *Brian Ferran*   55

Memories Of Rosemount
Boy's School – *Peter Gallagher*   59

Of Bulls, Bilberries And
Bygone Heroes – *Roy Hamilton*   62

"Maggie Magee Makes A
Good Cup Of Tea" – *Ann Hasson*   65

Happy Times – *Laurence Hasson*   67

"Peggy's Leg" And Rosemary Clooney
– *Maureen Hegarty*   68

From Donegal To Derry – *Danea Herron*   69

Growing Up In The Glen – *John Hume*   71

Snapshots – *John Keanie*   74

"Days Like This" – *Carita Kerr*   77

A Wonderful Place – *Geraldine McGrory*   80

A Place Of Which We Are Proud
– *Bishop James McGuinness*   81

'True And Trusty' – After Two Lads...
– *Gerard McChrystal*   82

20-a-side On The Streets Of Creggan
– *John O'Neill*   86

Rare Birds – *Anita Robinson*   87

Football And Cricket At Duncreggan Road
– *Claude Wilton*   89

NSPCC Foyle Children's Services

Lost childhood and innocence can never be regained. The hurt is particularly acute when it is stolen from the child through no fault of its own. The NSPCC Foyle Children's Resource Team work with children to help them overcome the harmful effects of abuse whether it is physical, emotional, sexual or neglect.

The scale of the problem is huge. The vast majority of the Team's recovery work is with victims traumatised by sexual abuse. All the children are referred to them by Social Services for their specialist service. They also facilitate self help groups for the parents of abused children.

One of the more positive aspects of the NSPCC's work involves the provision of day care facilities for preschool children, parenting skill's courses and "parent and toddler" groups. Playgroups in Irish Street and the Bogside in Derry City; and a facility in Strabane assists children and their families from the surrounding areas.

Another example of their pro-active approach is a special project to prevent children from one estate being caught up in the drugs scene.

It is important to remember that the abuse of children in our community is not limited to areas of social or economic deprivation. Children in all areas have suffered or are at risk. Problems exist even in rural areas.

Each year the NSPCC spend approximately £1.4 million to provide these services to abused children and their families in this area and throughout Northern Ireland. As 86% of the NSPCC's funding come from voluntary sources, your support in purchasing this book is greatly appreciated. Every penny donated or raised through fund-raising activities such as this book will be spent locally to the benefit of our children.

Introduction
Councillor Martin Bradley
Mayor

I congratulate Stephen Kelly, the Foyle District Committee of the NSPCC and Guildhall Press on producing this fine publication. Their hard work and effort is very evident and I would commend this book to you.

I was born in Creggan in 1964 and therefore grew up in what was perhaps the most troublesome 25 years in the history of our city.

The early 70s were, as we all know, extremely difficult times, but despite that, one of the most outstanding things about the people of Creggan and the people of Derry was their determination to maintain a sense of normality at all costs. Perhaps this explains why we have a ready sense of humour, it's almost like an in-built safety valve. We also had a tremendous civic pride and, despite the troubled years, I don't think any of us would have chosen to grow up anywhere other than in Derry.

The tireless work of all the staff of the NSPCC is greatly appreciated. Their skills and professionalism in this field are second to none. The task of piecing together, bit by bit, a shattered childhood must be daunting, but the NSPCC has shown through its many successes that this is possible.

Their work in developing child friendly communities; organising parenting skills courses; providing day care facilities; and, educating the public at large on the risks and dangers that children face has to be applauded.

I thank the NSPCC for its work for the children of our City and wish it and this publication every success.

Welcome

Lady Moyra Campbell, CVO
NSPCC Trustee

It is now over a century since the first NSPCC Office was opened in Derry, and the readiness of so many prominent and well-known citizens to contribute to this book is typical of the goodwill that the community has shown to our Society through the years.

My own early memories of the city are restricted to the highlight of our summer holidays, spent with my grandparents some twenty six miles away in Tyrone. This was the annual visit to Fosters, on the Strand, for a tea of a magic that later visits to patisseries in Paris or the Sacherhaus in Vienna have never been able to rival. The warm friendliness of those waitresses in their very smart uniforms, the huge variety of cakes with which they plied us, but above all, a wonderful dark syrupy lemonade of amazing fizziness, are as vivid in my mind today as when we faced the long drive home.

Tragically, for some in this great city, there is little to remember of security and happiness in childhood. The NSPCC's Foyle Children Resource Team exists to work with today's children who have suffered abuse or who are at risk, using their special skills to ensure that some of these children's memories will be transformed to happier ones. The proceeds of this book will help this work; I hope it has the greatest possible success.

Oh How Times Have Changed

Samuel Adair
Trade Unionist

When I was asked to recall my childhood memories of growing up in Derry I first of all could not believe that anyone would have the slightest interest as to what happened in Derry to someone like me all those years ago.

I often visit the place in which I was brought up – Ballyarnett on the outskirts of the city which I suppose one could say is no longer the outskirts. I recall with fondest memories my childhood there. My first real recollection is when we moved from Steelstown to Sandbank Cottages. The thrill of moving to a new house with 3 bedrooms and a living room and a massive sandpit at the back where scores and scores of youngsters and adults assembled to play football. Many an argument took place as to whether the ball crossed the line as we used our coats for goal posts.

I often recall my time spent at Ballyarnett School where the teachers in those days were Miss McCarter, Miss McKeen, Ted Maxwell and the Headmaster who was Mr Cooke. In those days if you were sent to see Mr Cooke you were certainly in difficulties. The school had a playground which was massive in our eyes but would be considered small by today's standards, together with a football pitch where we played football in the winter and cricket in the summer. Some of us thought we were the "Billy Wrights" and "Nat Lofthouse's" of those days.

We also had the racecourse and unbeknown to me I did not realise how much racecourses would mean to me in the future. In those days it was only athletes who ran round them and they were fondly described as the "harriers" who went round the 3 mile course almost every weekend. When the sandpit became overcrowded with too many people playing in it, it was decided to ask if any of the local farmers would allow us into one of their fields to play. Sir Basil McCorkell, who then had a massive house at Ballyarnett, kindly agreed to this provided that we used the gate and did not climb over the hedges. Youngsters came as far away as Burt in County Donegal and the surrounding areas to play in those fields. Everyone made their own fun in those days.

I always looked forward to the summertime in my youth as I had the opportunity to go for the 6 weeks holiday to my aunt and uncle in Carrigans in County Donegal. I was looked after by my aunt whom I thought the world of and my uncle until their deaths. I also fondly recall the times that we spent gathering potatoes as youngsters. In those days you would have got the almighty sum of two shillings and sixpence per day – the equivalent of 12½ new pence today. We thought we were well paid for doing that particular kind of work. There was many a day that we spent at Robert and Willie John Whylie's farm doing odd jobs, like rounding up the sheep and cows. We thought we were great people having the opportunity to do all of these things.

Times have changed. Around Sandbank now it is no longer the country as we knew it. It is now a built up area. In those days I can never recall a lock on the back door. It was always open. Friends and neighbours alike helped each other and formed what was then a strong community in that area. I can only look back with very fond memories of my childhood in Ballyarnett. I appreciate the upbringing by my mother and father and the influence both had on me as a child. They equipped me well for being brought up in a divided society such as Northern Ireland.

Eccentrics Or What?
Gerry Anderson
Broadcaster

Most people, when asked, say that they dream in black and white... a dream in colour is apparently comparatively rare. I'm sure there must be some perfectly adequate psychological reason for this but I wonder would it explain why I remember my childhood only in black and white.

I had a very happy childhood growing up in Derry in the fifties, but for reasons I can't fathom I don't remember any bright colours. Everything was grey, charcoal grey or black. Cars were black or grey, clothes were white, grey or black, buildings were grey and the people seemed happy and friendly, but still grey.

As I trawl my memory for a trace of colour, the only thing that comes to me are the bright colours of Gretta Torrens's parrot that used to sit in its cage outside her pet shop in Little James' Street and curse at the Scottish people who passed her door en route from the boat to the Lough Swilly bus station in Great James' Street. I think it was eventually brought permanently indoors at the behest of the RUC who received a number of complaints... the parrot spoke excellent Chaucerian English.

We used to buy new suits out of Burton's to wear for the closing of the annual retreat in St Eugene's Cathedral. We had a choice of three colours – black, charcoal grey and grey. I was an early dandy and always went for the exotic charcoal grey. I suppose it's not unusual really – nobody wore bright colours then. Maybe it was considered unmanly or slightly risqué. Bright coloured clothes couldn't be got anyway. At that time, if a man wanted to buy a red shirt he would probably have to fly to Naples.

I used to think about this quite a lot and just when I thought it was all just in my imagination, I saw an old photograph taken at the Brandywell of a crowd watching a football match in the thirties. There were thousands of people at the match, all wearing caps, and they seemed to be wearing identical clothes. Of course the photograph was in black and white, but you could tell that everybody was wearing dull clothes.

There was one startling exception. Standing in the front row of a section of the crowd was a figure who stood out immediately. Amid the homogeneous mass was a man dressed from head to toe in bright clothes – jumper, sports coat, cap, shoes, trousers and socks – all bright, but not seemingly all white, leading one to suspect that perhaps his jumper and socks and maybe his trousers were yellow or, who knows, may even be green or red!

I searched frantically for a name in the explanatory caption underneath and it read "Photograph taken at the Brandywell in 1938 featuring a large section of the crowd watching Derry City play Glenavon in a very well supported Irish League match. Prominent in the picture is the flamboyant figure of local eccentric Hawker Lynch".

So, there it was. You could tell he was an eccentric because he was wearing bright clothes. Maybe I was right after all – if you wore anything bright you were considered mad! Hawker Lynch wouldn't merit a second glance in the Brandywell this Sunday – he was ahead of his time.

I didn't know Hawker Lynch but I knew his sidekick, Johnny Cuttims, who survived up until comparatively recently. I was born and raised in Sackville Street and Johnny, for one reason or another, used to spend a lot of his time sitting alone on a doorstep at one of the entrances to Hogg & Mitchell's factory at the top of our street. He would sit there most nights not doing anything in particular and, being about 8 years old at the time, I was a little afraid of him as I used to have to pass him on my way back and forward to my Uncle James' sweet shop round the corner.

One winter's night about 9 o'clock I edged nervously past him and he called me over. "C'mere young fella" he said. (I've shortened this for obvious reasons. Those of you who remember Johnny Cuttims' severe speech impediment, will realise that the act of saying "C'mere young fella" took a considerable amount of time and effort.) "Look at that moon" he said, gazing skywards. I did what I was told with some trepidation. "It's a full moon" he said. "You can make out every feature with your naked eye. Do you believe in the man in the moon?" "I never thought about it much" I stuttered truthfully. "Well you should" he said. "If there was a man in the moon he'd have to have food to live on, wouldn't he?" "Yes, I suppose he would" I answered. "Well, use your imagination. Look at the moon and tell me if there's anything there that looks like food". I looked at the moon. It was huge. "Look over to the left hand side, near the top. Does that not look like an apple tree to you?" I looked hard. He was right. There was a kind of outline thing that did vaguely resemble a tree or plant. I told him so. "There you are" he laughed. "Now look down at the bottom right hand side. Couldn't that be a rabbit?" You know, I could see something that looked a bit like something on four legs. "That's the man in the moon off to a good start. Plenty of apples and a bit of rabbit for his dinner" Johnny said, warming to the exercise.

He went on to point out other imaginary objects that he saw on the surface of the lunar landscape that could be of use to the man in the moon and I found myself sitting down beside him on the doorstep looking for something on the surface that had escaped his attention. We sat there talking for an hour until I heard the voice of my mother calling me. I had been sent out for a pint of milk and this was no way to go about it. I tore myself away, bought the milk, and said good night to him on my way back home. He nodded, waved airily and stared at the moon again.

I didn't think about it much at the time but now I realise that Johnny Cuttims had made me study the surface of the moon as I had never studied it before. Of course, he was only an eccentric... just like his mate, Hawker Lynch.

The White Horse Inn
Colum Arbuckle
Radio Producer

The White Horse Inn at Campsie has been a familiar landmark to travellers of the main Derry to Limavady road for centuries, but on the 1st of June 1948 it was quite a different place to the prestigious hotel we know today. That was the date my father, mother and myself took up residence in the old Inn which had been on the site for centuries. It was just before my first birthday and for my parents, who had been living in rented rooms since they got married, it seemed like a dream come true. My father was a barman by trade and after he served his time in John O'Donnell's Ulster House he was looking around for a better position.

"The job was advertised in the Derry Journal", he recalls, "and it said that there was a free house with it so I applied and after being interviewed by Johnny Whiteside, who was the owner at the time, and Father Kielt who, I suppose, was looking for a barman of the proper character, I got the position of resident barman of The White Horse Inn at £4 a week."

The original Inn had for hundreds of years been a stopping place for horse-drawn coaches on their way to and from Derry and Coleraine, and in its day was probably quite a luxurious dwelling. Passengers could get a rest, a bite to eat and a drink in the bar while waiting for the horses to be changed. This building was our free house which came with the job but, as it turned out, it wasn't quite what we had expected on first reading the advertisement.

There was another family, the Cookes, living in it. They lived upstairs and we had two rooms and a shared kitchen and hall downstairs. The structure of the building hadn't changed much since the coaching days but it was nearing the end of its days and looked it. There was no running water, no electricity and the only heat was from a big open fire in the living room. Light was provided by an old Tilly lamp which had to be refilled with paraffin oil and primed two or three times before bedtime on winter evenings.

The bar was lit by gas lights from bottled gas and glasses had to be washed under a cold tap in the back yard. The toilet for both the house and bar was a primitive outside dry affair consisting of little more than a wall for the gentlemen and a bucket for the ladies.

The bar opened from 10.00am in the morning to 9.00pm in the evening but closed for an hour at 6.00pm while my father got his tea and, because he was working a six day week and was entitled to one half day, it closed on a Tuesday at 2.00pm. Any locals who wanted sustenance on a Tuesday evening had to go further afield. Stout, from bottles only, was one shilling – sixpence cheaper than the return bus fare to Derry.

It sounds like a pretty primitive place to live in and, I suppose by today's standards, it was. But expectations were not as high then and when you compare it to living in one room in a two-up two-down terraced house in the middle of the city, the space, privacy and freedom of a country house with your livelihood right next door must have, to my parents, seemed a pretty attractive lifestyle indeed.

"Do you know this? Six years we lived there and it was really the happiest years of my life" my mother will tell you to this day. "There was something exciting going on in it every day. The people in the neighbourhood were the friendliest I had ever met. We came into it as strangers and we were just made at home. Every house we went to we were treated like royalty. Everybody made that much of you. I tried to make the house as comfortable as possible and while Joe was working the bar I decorated the rooms as best I could. I scraped away the old lime from the walls and then papered them, and got some plywood from a man down the road and got the old kitchen panelled."

"The door was never locked", dad recollects, "and the house never emptied. As often as not when I closed the bar at tea-time any customers who were still there would come in and join us for a bite to eat. Most of the locals who were coming or going on the Derry bus or just passing by on their way to the shops in Eglinton, would drop into the house for a cup of tea and even at night, after the bar closed, few would go home before calling in for a chat. One thing I was very strict about was the bar licensing laws and there was never any drink sold outside opening hours, nor was there ever any drink allowed in the house. I remember one time two policemen came to the door about ten o'clock at night and said they had information that illegal drinking was going on in the house. I brought them in and there were about half a dozen men sitting around the big table eating soup. The policemen looked around and satisfied themselves that nothing was going on and were about to leave when the sergeant asked me what the lovely smell was. That's Kathleen's soup, I told him, would you like some? 'I would' said he, and joined us for a bowl before heading back on duty".

I don't remember too much about the first couple of years in the Inn but I certainly have many memories of later times. It was a magical place for a young boy with a vivid imagination. In the old stables, still there from the coaching days, bandits and ghouls lurked on dark days and on brighter ones, camp could be made with fellow cowboys or Roman forts could be defended against barbarian invaders. The garden was huge and contained all sorts of fruits like gooseberries, raspberries, apples, pears and plums. Climbing and swinging apparatus were constructed on the many trees using old bits of harness and pieces of broken stout crates. The Black Braes wasn't far away – as exciting to me then as any Continental seaside is to today's youngsters.

We always had a dog and for a while I had a pet piglet. It would follow me around everywhere and come when called, just like a pup. It even pulled a 'chariot' down the garden on a couple of occasions. Someone had given it to my mother to fatten and get ready to sell for slaughter, but by the time it had reached the desired weight it was so tame that no-one had the heart to send it to its predestined fate. It stayed with us until we got a farmer to take it. Of course he had to promise not to kill it before it was allowed to leave The White Horse Inn.

It all sounds like an idyllic country life meandering through the hours, days and weeks at the pace of a lazy meadow-stream. Not a bit of it according to my mother. At Campsie even getting in the weekly groceries was a complicated affair. "I had to phone the XL Stores in Derry from the pay phone in the bar and they would deliver them the next time the van was in the area. The All Cash Store mobile shop would also come around on a Tuesday and a Friday, and occasionally Quiggs would come around with fruit and vegetables. We got our milk, eggs and potatoes from Lowery's farm across the road. Sam Lowery was a preacher and would just as soon deliver a sermon as a ticking off to his workers. The potato-pickers liked the sermons better as it gave them a brief rest from their back-breaking work".

There was never a dull moment in the bar. The customers were a strange mixture of locals and British Army, Navy and Air Force personnel from the nearby married quarters. In the evening most would arrive on bicycles which they leaned three and four deep outside the bar and the house. At closing time sorting out who owned which bicycle often led to minor altercations.

There was no form of heating in the public house except a coal fire, but Johnny Whiteside wouldn't buy coal for it. "Joe has plenty there on the top shelf to keep you warm" he would say if anyone complained.

My dad was involved in an elaborate deception one evening which not only fooled the drinkers but also half of Campsie and a good portion of the residents of Eglinton village.

"There was a character who used to frequent the bar who fancied himself as a bit of a ladies man but he had been a bit down on his romantic luck for a few years and was constantly being teased by the locals. He decided that it was time to re-establish his reputation so he enlisted my help in an elaborate plot which had to be carried out with split-second timing to make it work. He passed the word around that he had a date with a beautiful woman but he refused to reveal anything about her except that he was to meet her outside the White Horse at eight o'clock one summer evening. He positioned himself outside the bar at about quarter to eight and, of course, anyone who was inside came out to see who this mystery woman was. I was well out of sight down the Donnybrewer Road dressed as a woman. I was small and of slight build so I was able to get away with it. On the stroke of eight I mounted a borrowed ladies bike, cycled around the corner into full view of the waiting onlookers. As soon as our man saw me he jumped on his bike and the two of us cycled off as fast as we could towards Eglinton. When we got there we did a couple of circuits of the village before we disappeared. He went back home by a different route and I managed to slip back to the bar and get changed. It was years after before anyone realised they had all been fooled".

There was another occasion when one of the bar patrons dressed up as a woman and tried to scare some of the men going outside to the toilet by pretending to be a ghostly apparition. Many would say though that there were already enough unearthly spirits around the White Horse Inn without someone having to act the part. Most locals would swear the building was haunted.

One night, just about a year before we moved in, there were a number of men playing cards around the big table in the front room. A round was dealt but every card inexplicably fell face up. The players, and this story was told to mum and dad directly by them for they still drank in the bar, tried again but the same thing happened. They dealt a third hand but when the cards again landed all face up the men lifted the deck and without saying a word to each other left the Inn. Cards were never again played around that table nor in that room.

While we were living in the house we were being constantly asked about ghosts and there were even occasions when people gathered outside to try and catch a glimpse of a horse-drawn carriage which was said to appear at certain times of the year. We saw nor heard anything at all until one cold winter's night when we were sure that the devil himself had come to sup at The White Horse Inn.

When my mother tells the tale it can still bring a chill over the cosiest of company. "Well that night... I'll never forget it. We were terrorised and so were George and Mary Cooke up the stairs. I heard what I thought was like a step ... first in the hall. I wakened Joe. Then it went up the stairs ... thump ... thump ... thump ... very slow. When it got to the top it came down again ...

step ... step ... step. Joe wouldn't get up and neither would George up the stairs. Not one of us would get up to look. We were all riveted to our beds. The next morning the mystery of the night visitor was revealed when a large potato, half-eaten by a rat, was found lying in the hall at the bottom of the stairs. The rodent had obviously been trying to get the spud to some secluded part of the house and had managed to lift it up the stairs step by step ... thump ... thump ... thump... and just when it got it to the top of the staircase it lost control and it bounced back down again ... step ... step ... step."

That rat wasn't the only one to give us grief in the old house. The place was infested by them and we all had many a close encounter. Mum trapped one behind a cupboard one time and managed to 'spear' it with a poker. She thought it was dead but as soon as she withdrew the weapon it jumped down and scuttled towards the back door only to meet a swift end in the jaws of the family dog. They had a particular liking for a cavity behind the big open fireplace. At night you could see them running between holes in the back of the grate and in the garden at night they could be heard scurrying to their hiding places as soon as the back door opened.

Someone told my dad once that if you burned a rat alive its squeals during its death throws would drive the others away. He caught one in a cage and roasted it on a bonfire just outside the back door. The ritual didn't work and he told me years later, "It was the cruellest thing I ever done".

Like the unfortunate creature we all nearly met untimely ends during our stay at the White Horse. I came close on two occasions. The first time was when a large delivery lorry missed me by inches as it sped along the main road. The second time was inside the house but was no less dramatic. I was in bed in the back bedroom ill at the time and the ceiling, an old heavy plaster and lath affair, fell in around me. The first part blocked the door from the inside and my mother couldn't get to me. She ran to the bar to get help and some men managed to get the back window open and pass me out through it seconds before the whole lot came down on top of the bed. Mum always said that if I had not been rescued when I was "I would never have spoke."

Her near encounter with the grim reaper happened one Christmas Eve when she was seven months pregnant with my sister Siobhan. My father was in bed very ill and that morning she had just about managed to get the heavy front shutters off, open the bar and hold the fort until a replacement barman arrived. Later she was down in the front room, standing on the big table to hang some washing up on an inside line. This was the same table that had been the scene of the card players eerie experience some years earlier. When she was getting down she fell and landed on her back on the old flagstone floor. She couldn't get to her feet and dad was so ill that he was unable to rise out of bed to assist. The Cookes upstairs had a radio on and didn't hear her cries for help. She had to crawl on her hands and knees back to the kitchen and somehow manage to pull herself up on a chair. She was so badly hurt, however, that she couldn't even go to the fire and remove a pot of tapioca that she had boiling there. She had no option but to sit and watch it boil in and burn the pot.

Later that day she had recovered sufficiently to go to the bar and call the doctor. Fortunately she had suffered no damage to her pregnancy and nothing was broken, but dad on the other hand was, by this time, very seriously ill and the doctor suspected meningitis. He wanted to shift him into the hospital but because it was Christmas Eve he decided to wait. "That was the loneliest Christmas I ever had" mum remembers. "We had planned to spend the holidays with my mother, Colum's granny, in Donegal and Santa had been instructed to deliver his presents there. I hadn't one bite to eat in the house and practically no money to get anything even if I had been able to go shopping. I did try and get a chicken but there were just none available. I didn't know what I was going to do but luckily a regular in the bar heard of my plight and offered me a duck which I was glad to accept. Colum took sick that evening also and I sat by myself on Christmas Day eating the duck with the tears blinding me". Dad was shifted into hospital on Boxing Day and thankfully recovered. Siobhan was delivered with no complications the following February. She wasn't born in the White Horse but she was the last newborn baby to be brought into it.

In 1954 my father was offered a better paying job in Ebrington House in the Waterside and we had to give up the country residence. We left on 1st June 1954 exactly six years to the day from the date we moved in. We went from the spacious 'luxury' of The White Horse Inn to one room at number 7 Limavady Road, the winter residence of Cullen's Amusements. For me, a boisterous seven year old, it was like leaving one Disney World and finding another one just around the corner. But that is another story.

"It's Never Too Late To Have A Happy Childhood"

Roy Arbuckle
Write, Singer and Songwriter

I was born on Bennett Street
Slipping sliding down
To Abercorn Road, and the long fall
To Foyle Road and the railway line.

Number 2, Upper Bennett Street huddled against the jail wall. Small and dark, two rooms, one storey, toilet in the back yard. My mother was from the Fountain, my father from Ivy Terrace. People didn't move far from their roots those days. We moved when I was six. Some of my memories of Bennett Street are borrowed, mostly from my mother. When Brian Friel first came to public attention, my mother told me that every time I went missing as a toddler I would be found in Brian Friel's house with his mother. They lived close to the McLaughlins, Teddy, Dessie and Elma and Liam. Next door to us were the Warkes. The Arbuckles and the Warkes had the distinction of being the two largest families in the new Fountain Estate when we all moved up there in 1950. Ten Arbuckles and Fourteen Warkes, good Protestant families! Recently both David Warke and I came into possession of an old photograph of Bennett Street. It's important to me, framed on my kitchen wall, and Davy Warke has done the same. I find it a bit strange that we both have an attachment to Bennett Street, given that we were living in what were basically hovels, damp, cold, overcrowded, no electricity and a zinc bath in front of the fire. I still look at the spot where the house was every time I drive up Abercorn Road. There's nice new houses now and the Abercorn Bar is much extended from the original 'Wine and Spirit Store' of those days.

I have two vivid memories of Bennett Street; the first a vision of a large carthorse having a pee in the street. To my two or three year old eyes it was incredible that so much pee could come out of anything, a river, torrent, heading for the gutter and Abercorn Road. The other picture is of the large pink bloomers of Miss Pollock as she sat at her desk in front of the one room school in Lower Bennett Street. I think I only spent one term there before moving to the Model. There are fleeting visions of my cousin Betty washing my hair with strong fingers in the zinc bath in front of the fire and the faint embarrassment of that. I can remember my sisters making beds and trying not to break the gas mantle. Breaking the delicate mantles seemed to be a really bad and expensive thing to do. Psychologists say that the first three years of our lives set the pattern for the rest. I wonder what my memories say about me. Pee, bloomers, baths, beds and a dread about the price of things. Hmmm.

There was a man who used to walk down Abercorn Road. He was big, with wild eyes and hair and staggered as he walked. He wore a fawn coloured raincoat and obviously didn't like the stares and scared whisperings. 'He's drunk' some of the older children volunteered. Years later I found out that he was 'Shell Shocked' – one of the walking wounded of the Second World War. I can still see his wild eyes.

Bennett Street, Ivy Terrace and the Fountain were all as much a part of my childhood as the Northland Estate. There were regular visits to the grannies at number 7 Ivy Terrace and McLaughlin's in Joseph Place. The Life Boys in First Derry Church and the Boy Scouts in St Augustines. Bonfires and bangers, rock'n'roll on a Dansette record player in the Fountain on the 11th nights. George Ferguson's for a crew cut, Sandy McGowan's for sweets and the delectable Rita Gardiner in the house next door. Even though we had moved our social life was centred round the Fountain.

I remember the first day in number 11 Northland Parade. Stairs! We ran up and down the bare wooden stairs until my already distracted mother screamed enough. In our first year there I fell off some paving stones and fractured my arm. A plaster of paris in the City and County Hospital and weeks of itching.

In 1952, Coronation year, I got my first money for singing. A street party had been arranged and when it rained the party moved to the Epworth Hall. Tommy Craig and the local postman, trying to keep dozens of kids amused, offered me half a crown to sing and I did. I can't remember what I sang but the half crown stuck in my mind. Another public appearance around that time was singing 'In The Deep Midwinter' at the Nativity play performed by Life Boys in First Derry. Helen Dickson gave me the choice of singing solo or dressing up as an angel. I sang.

Another memory of this time was being in the guard of honour for the new Queen when she came to Brooke Park. We little Life Boys stood for what seemed like hours until a big black car wooshed past carrying its Royal cargo. 'Was that it?' I thought. In the Model School we had Empire Day every year. It consisted of the whole school assembling in the playground and singing Rule Britannia and Land Of Hope And Glory. I suppose Britannia did rule the waves and the sun never set on the British Empire in the fifties. Changed times.

Writing this, especially for the NSPCC, makes me ask myself a question. Did I have a deprived childhood? I surely did, if you measure deprivation by economic standards. The price of a gas mantle striking fear in the heart. I really wonder how my mother managed. If you measure a happy childhood by feelings of warmth and security and richness of experience and the safety of belonging to a tight community I was very lucky. The streets, our playground, were safe. We could wander and explore, walk anywhere any time, traffic hadn't really been invented. We could get on a pram wheeled cart on Park Avenue and career down Academy Road, Northland Parade, a wee bit of Northland Avenue, then Northland Terrace, turning right on Argyle Street and left on Northland Road for the final rush down Rock Road, skidding to a stop outside Hunters Bakery where the long pull back to Park Avenue began. I know that it wasn't so good for a lot of families, alcoholism and family violence were around, but thank God, not in my house.

I started making money for myself when I was about 12, delivering groceries on a message bike for John Lovett in Edenmore Street. I suppose that couldn't happen today, child labour laws being what they are. Later I got up at 4.00am three mornings a week to deliver the Derry Standard round the city centre shops in all weathers. That was hard for someone who loves his bed as much as me.

I suppose the greatest legacy of my childhood is an overbearing poverty consciousness and undervaluing of myself which I am sill in the process of changing. These days, whenever I get caught up in bitterness about the lack of money and opportunity in my youth, I always come back to a bumper sticker I saw once... "It's never too late to have a happy childhood."

Anybody got a toffee apple? Brandy Ball? McGowan's Highland Toffee?

Memories of Nellie Ramsey, Gacka Wacka And The Palace

Jimmy Cadden
Editor, Londonderry Sentinel

The wanes of today may think they live in a Derry which is vibrant and alive. They may feel they can shop in ultra modern malls and that they eat and drink in superb pubs and clubs, and they are right to think that. But what they cannot do is compare the quality of life to the Derry of the sixties and seventies with that of today. You see, what they miss out on today is held very dearly by people like me.

The child of the nineties cannot take a trip down William Street and stroll through Nellie Ramsey's.

The child of the nineties cannot spend a few minutes in the hilarious company of Gacka Wacka.

Nor can they spend a few hours watching Jerry Lewis or Elvis Presley in the City or The Palace.

Nor can they sample the special atmosphere that was Brandywell when Linfield came to visit.

I well remember walking with my father and grandfather to the Brandywell on these big match days. I found it hard to work out just why the visiting supporters were singing "The Sash" as they trooped up Carlisle Road. After all, wasn't this my song?

I remember telling the headmaster of the then Foyle College that I had suddenly taken violently ill one wet Thursday afternoon. To this day, I would swear he didn't believe me, but he couldn't take a chance. He told me to go home and go straight to bed. I went out of the school gates and went straight to Brandywell, where Derry City were meeting Wolverhampton Wanders in a Texaco Cup fixture.

Money for a child from Irish Street in the sixties and seventies was always tight, but when a seemingly rich American aunt arrived for a holiday, well, it was The Twelfth, Christmas and a birthday all rolled into one. "Take Chris and Jane (my two Yankee cousins) over town and get something for y'all with this." She had given me a fiver, which in today's currency would be like handing a child of the nineties £50! What did we buy? "We" bought nothing, for here at last was the chance for me to fulfil a lifelong (12 years) ambition.

I took all three of us to Strand Road, and Willman's Hairdressers. After swearing Chris and Jane to solemn silence – a silence they held for all of thirty seconds when we finally got back home – I proudly walked into Willman's and paid £5 to have my embarrassingly curly hair straightened out. The new hair style lasted all of twenty-four hours, much shorter than the pain in my rear end, a result of a severe leathering with a wooden spoon, held firmly in the hands of my mother.

But even in those days, the sectarianism which so pervades our society today existed. I remember walking home along Northland Road, after a rather late rugby practice at the Foyle College pitches. As I approached the junction with Eden Terrace, I was stopped by a gang of three lads, whose ages ranged from ten to fifteen. Now wearing a Foyle College blazer in those days was a rather obvious giveaway as to with which foot you kicked. So as the lads came nearer to me, I wrapped my raincoat tightly around the crimson blazer.

"Wha futball team dae yae follow?" they asked. "Spurs," says I, feeling mildly content that I had got round the problem. "Don't be cute," said they, "Wha team in Scotlan?" Now this was altogether a different state of affairs. They clearly wanted me to say Rangers or Celtic. One answer would have given me a good hiding, the other would probably not have been believed anyway, once they saw my coat. Summoning up the last ounce of inventiveness I had, I replied: "Falkirk!" "Leave im alone," says one of my would be attackers. "He's wan o them smart ones that goes tae Foyle. They know nathin about football. They play that cissie's game – rugby." Off into the gloom they went, as I walked so quickly away in relief that six minutes later I was in Guildhall Square, waiting for a Waterside bus.

Finally, let me relate my favourite trips of those days. They were the Sunday School excursions to Portrush. The excitement of waiting with bucket and spade, usually as the rain fell from the heavens, at the station platform, is still a feeling I can remember. I can also remember waiting in the queue at the hall in Kerr Street in Portrush for the cup of tea and bag of buns, which contained two soggy and dog-eared sandwiches and a small bun with a wee bit of white or pink icing on top. Then it was down to Barry's for a run on the helter-skelter and a trip on the ghost train, before buying the obligatory water pistol for the journey home on the train.

This may not sound very grand or exciting to a child of today, but to me it was brilliant, exciting and the stuff of memories which will live with me to the grave.

Compare the two eras?

There is no comparison!

Mr Stephen Kelly,
NSPCC Foyle Children's Services
29a Strand Road,
Derry BT48 7BC
Northern Ireland

21st August, 1997

Dear Stephen,

Thank you for the invitation to contribute to your planned book "Memories Of Derry".

I am more than happy to support the project, and I believe the most significant gesture I can make is to give you my personal authorisation to use the words of "The Town I Loved So Well", waiving any and all fees and copyright income. This piece of work is very special to me, as you might imagine, and is as autobiographical as I have ever allowed myself to get in a song!

I was very fortunate in having a particularly happy childhood growing up in Derry, one of the reasons, I'm sure, why the place has always been so important to me.

I was devastated to learn of the number of children in my home town today who will have memories of _their_ childhood which will be far from happy. To hear that two of the largest child sex abuse rings in the UK were recently uncovered in Derry just makes my blood run cold. It certainly shatters that comfortable notion that such depravity could never happen in a close, God fearing community like ours.

My heart bleeds for the victims and their families and I am lost in admiration for the unsung heroes, the counsellors in the NSPCC, who have been working tirelessly with these victims to help them rebuild their lives. They certainly deserve our recognition, our respect and our support. It's the least we can do as a community.

I wish you great success in your work and if there is anything I can do to help in the future, please do not hesitate to ask.

Sincerely,
Phil Coulter

The Town I Loved so Well

In my memory, I will always see
The town that I have loved so well,
Where our school played ball by the gas-yard wall
and we laughed through the smoke and the smell.
Going home in the rain, running up the dark lane
Past the Gaol and down behind the Fountain,
those were happy days, in so many, many ways
In the town I loved so well.

In the early morn the shirt factory's horn
Called women from the Creggan, the Moor and the Bog;
While the men on the dole played a mothers' role
Fed the children, and then walked the dog.
And when times got tough, there was just about enough
And they saw it through without complaining:
For deep inside was a burning pride
In the town I loved so well.

There was music there in the Derry air
Like a language that we all could understand;
I remember the day that I earned my first pay
When I played in a small pick-up band.
There I spent my youth, and to tell you the truth
I was sad to leave it all behind me:
For I'd learned about life, and I'd found a wife
In the town I loved so well.

But when I returned, how my eyes have burned
To see how a town could be brought to its knees
By the armoured cars and the bombed-out bars,
And the gas that hangs onto every breeze.
Now the Army's installed by that old gas-yard wall
And the damned barbed wire gets higher and higher:
With their tanks and guns, Oh my God, what have they done
to the town I Loved so Well?

Now the music's gone, but they carry on
For their spirit's been bruised, never broken
They will not forget, but their hearts are set
On tomorrow and peace once again.
For what's done is done, and what's won is won;
and what's lost is lost and gone forever:
I can only pray for a bright, brand new day
In the Town I Loved So Well.

Words and music – Phil Coulter
© 1973 for the World – Four Seasons Music Ltd

The Sticks
Jim Craig
Teacher

Money was scarce in Creggan in the Fifties. It was even scarcer for us children. Pocket money was what you read about in the Enid Blyton books in the Brooke Park Library. Money came to us, apart from First Communion and Confirmation, by way of windfalls; lucky breaks as unpredictable as a lotto win or the teacher's temper. Windfalls like a generous aunt visiting, a letter for your birthday from your godfather in America, a passing drunk man, a tanner found in the gutter or Granny and Granda on pension day, these were all breaks that were thrilling but totally undependable. Coppers or silver were better from these sources than notes. Notes were always taken off you in case you lost them. In case? You just had.

But these lucky breaks were too erratic. What was needed was a steady job which would ensure a regular income especially in the dog days of summer. In the holidays that marked my leaving primary school, seven of us went into serious conference at the gable end of our house in Malin Gardens. Those present were; Kevin, Robert, Tony, John, Christy, Dessie and myself. Item No 1 on the agenda, how to make money. Real money.

The frivolous, outlandish and downright criminal ideas were ruled out first. Selling the Guildhall to Yankee sailors, taking the Mayor hostage, robbing the manager of the Sackville Street National Bank with our Tony's really "true to life" gun... that sort of thing were all fully discussed but fortunately rejected. Also discussed; showing films in somebody's hall... but Fr Carolan was at that already. Forming a show band... none of us could really play anything but that had not stopped a lot of other Derry bands. Selling tickets for a raffle... but we had no money to buy the first prize never mind the fourth prize. Then Robert and Christy were called in for their tea. The meeting ended at six-thirty without any definite conclusion being reached.

By the next day I had cracked it. Sell sticks. Sure everybody in Creggan had to light a fire. We had Dessie's wee cart, my father had a hatchet and Robert's father had a pile of old timber lying in the back yard. The idea took off. The boys were excited and soon it was all systems go. In Robert's yard we were chopping, bundling, tying and stacking Dessie's wee cart. Heated discussions were held on price. Must be cheaper than the shops but still enough to make a profit. Thatcherites had nothing to teach us boys. Our target market was to be the streets immediately adjacent to Malin Gardens, Dunmore, Leenan, Inishowen, Dawros, Lower Greenwalk. Not Melmore, there was a big mad dog up there that took lump out of one of the Harkins and he had to go to the City and County. Robert's wee brother who wanted to be cut in was ruled out. He gleefully pointed out that only eejits and gacks would try to sell sticks in the summer.

We prayed for cold and rain and thanked God when we got both. John and Tony were on chopping and Kevin and Christy were on tying, "Don't make them too fat." Robert and Dessie were put on sales because Robert could put on good manners and it was Dessie's cart after all. I was in charge of money and looking out for other free sources of timber.

By tea-time we had chopped all Robert's da's wood and even better sold all our sticks. We had 17/6 in the kitty. A big row broke out among the workers. Some (Tony, John and Christy) wanted to go for fish suppers and lemonade right away. Others (Dessie, Kevin and Robert) said no we should keep our money for payday like proper people in the real world. My casting vote was with the payday group. I let them all count the money and then wrote it in my little notebook in joined up writing and got everybody to sign their names to it. Not everybody could do joined up writing I noticed.

Next day I went out on a recky. I spotted a dead tree in the grounds of the Priest's house. We held a quick meeting in Kevin's front hall, got a few ropes, the loan of Doherty's big hatchet, and the whole production team were diverted to the dead tree site. Christy was left to keep an eye out for parents or the police. The hacking and pulling began, so did the cursing. John warned us "No cruising".

He had just made his confirmation and was heavy into holiness and good living and all that stuff. The hacking was going well when Christy called "Cops! Cops!" The hatchets were fired into the undergrowth quickly followed by all of us.

"Where's the cops?"
"Coming up Beechwood".
"How many of them?"
"Just the one".
Just the one?"
Where is he now?"
"There."
"Ach wise up that's not a cop, it's my da in his busman's uniform."
"Aye, I thought he looked a bit wee."

"Watch it! he's still my da – anyway he's bigger than your da".

"Let's go".

"Naw – if my da sees me I'll be brought in and I might as well be in jail then".

When my father passed we emerged. The tree eventually fell. Tony, the big expert on films called out, "Timber" and Dessie got confused and called out "There she blows"!

We had not thought this through properly – the tree was down but how were we to get it home? Dessie's wee cart was useless. We tried dragging it – no good. Then John remembered a cart that was always sitting at the gable of a house in the Brandywell. "What use is a cart without a horse?" asked Tony.

Another argument began. Christy and Tony wanted their money right away and headed off home in a huff. John being big on religion called me, "Judas."

"I never kissed nobody" said I.

"Naw, but you hold the money."

"What's he on about?" asked Kevin.

The firm was falling apart. Dessie and Robert said they'd go and see about transport.

An hour later things had simmered down. Kevin, Tony, John, Christy and myself sat under Quigley's lamppost wondering where Dessie and Robert had got to!

We were despondent, we didn't even care if the Rosemount crowd stole our tree for their bonfire. I would divide out the money and think of something else to raise cash. Go solo and avoid disputes and threatened strikes.

We had begun to speculate in a desultory way when our reverie was shattered by a commotion on Broadway. Crowds of cheering, prancing children laughing, calling, waving, ran in front, beside and behind a donkey. "The entry into Jerusalem." said John.

Dessie was at the front of this noisy procession leading the donkey. Robert was perched on its back, waving triumphantly to his followers. We hared over to this mad throng.

"Where did you get the donkey?"

"It's mine. I found it."

"You found it?"

"Aye, it was just standing in the middle of the field. Nobody was near it! Where's the cart, we're in business!"

"Cops! Cops!" called Kevin and it wasn't my father this time.

The police found the donkey standing in the middle of Broadway. Nobody was near it.

Coming Home
Peter Cunnah
Lead Vocalist – D:ream

Strangely coincidental that a request for a small contribution of my childhood memories comes after a recent trip to Derry. My visits home are sadly too infrequent and are often grabbed moments of opportunity. This particular time I drove from London to Derry with my girlfriend Amy and our baby substitute Dusky; he's big, black, with huge teeth and definitely Alsatian.

As always on our arrival home Mum was under orders to have enough stew on the boil to feed half of Africa. Stew being the kind of meal you can stretch out over several days without losing interest.

Dad, who displays most men's obsession with technology has just bought the biggest television I have ever seen – I'm sure it's over 45 inches. I'm suspicious the idea came after his last stay with us in London when he took a great shine to my modest 35 incher. I'm now looking into the possibility of a complete home cinema system and will keep you posted.

Girlfriends and mothers have a penchant for rooting through old baby photographs and I have in the course of my life endured the usual comments and embarrassments, even on national TV. So I avoid the issue by making drinks while they compare notes like a pair of genetic scientists attempting to predict the future. Colour of father's eyes; blue. Plus wife to be's eyes; brown. Equals... Well you get the picture.

Come to that dad just happens to have had all the family standard 8 home movies, featuring yours truly, transferred to video. Brilliant, now I can spend one blissful week caught in the debate over which direction any future children's hair may part. Mine naturally parts to the left (I'm convinced that this is an inherited trait as I picture generations of paddies walking to the church/pub/work with their wives fashion tip of the day firmly marked on their scalps and hence passed on to me).

It's not quite Blade Runner the Directors Cut but makes strangely interesting viewing. Here's wee baby Peter aged 8 weeks looking like any tiny baby does to an adult male (something between an orang-utan and a wrinkled prune). Born into this world 30 August 1966. The Beatles had just released Rubber Soul and this probably explains where I got mine.

One of the most prevailing memories I have of Derry as a child is my gypsy spirit taking flight from Dove Gardens in completely the wrong direction aged 3 in search of my Aunt Kathleen coming home from the Star factory. Three quarters of a mile later two kind men in their blue Capri stopped me and as I was able to give them my name and address they promptly returned me to my mother's abundant thanks, and now mine. Needless to say that's why I drove over this trip, instead of dealing with the map. Never ever ask me to navigate, I still have problems telling stage left from right.

Ah, now we've come to the 'I can recognise myself in those videos' stage; torturing my cousin Paul Condren at Fahan beach. Oh and there's one of me with my granny Cassy McDowell. That's the McDowell's from Union Street. I'm reminded of the story of how mum met dad. She was a local girl, the youngest of thirteen. He was based in Derry but came from Manchester, a Royal Navy guy. She a Catholic, he a Protestant. But love knows no bounds and they were wed within six months.

Dad changed religion to marry mum and I was baptised Catholic. I guess because of them I was reared almost neutral with a balanced outlook on the troubles. I avoided being indoctrinated into one camp or the other and now sit firmly on the fence. Keep your mouth shut, say nothing, stay out of trouble, avoid standing near windows during a riot. Essential survival tactics in a war zone. All I've known my whole life is the troubles and still to this day I don't have any answers. Like most I'm dismayed but powerless.

The on-screen footage is amazing, seeing my parents roughly the same age I am now (31 for those curious enough), carting me around various locations with dad looking like Kirk Douglas and mum like Jackie Kennedy. Cool Couple. It really brings it home to me just how short life is and how time flies. The video has already closed its last chapter on Butlins '69 and it's time for another cup of tea.

Aged 5 we moved to Carnhill where I attended St Patrick's, Pennyburn. These were happy days where boys separated from girls around the age of primary three. I often joke that this could have been part of some master plan to avoid juvenile pregnancies or at least to give both sexes an equal amount of socio-sexually regressive behaviour in later life.

Frighteningly we reach that period of time that most people in their thirties dread to think they lived through; the 70s. I marvel at the size of those flares and that haircut, now come full circle and back in fashion. I hate to say it but at a time when a pair of Bay City Rollers checked trousers were every child's dream, I got off lightly with a pair of gingham (Rupert the Bear) flares. I got ample chance later in life to re-address the injustice with D:ream.

The videos are now over and I breathe a sigh of relief. But when all's been said and done I can't think of a more happy place to have grown up in than

Derry. Home for me is a community with real hardships but masses of love.

When I look at the plight of children around the world and even on our own doorstep I thank God, my parents, and my lucky stars I was reared there.

Dad's got the video camera out and it's time to create some new memories – were off to Fahan. Mum, Dad, Amy, me and our 18 month old boy Dusky.

People

Witness here from exodus an islands loving prodigals
Returned from foreign shores they wonder what in hell's going on
Destruction n' pointless violence affecting all of you and me
While innocents like pawns kneel down to close their hands and pray
Give us hope of a peaceable solution
We'll lose our chance if we go too far
People let me ask you who is right and who is wrong
People if peace is dying who will answer our children
How I know you How I know you How I know you
Misguided sons of twisted hearts Abusing power to their gain
While braver men die fighting using words as swords they say
Shrouded hate in controversy feeds the media and divides
How strange I feel a stranger in the homeland of my mind
Always hope of a peaceful revolution
Our day has come we've come so far
People let me ask you who is right and who is wrong
People if peace is dying who will answer our children
How I know you How I know you How I know you
So we gotta turn around and make the future a brighter day
So we gotta turn around Loves gotta make a stand
And so are we to turn around and make the future a brighter day
People get a change of heart loves gonna make it happen
People let me ask you who is right and who is wrong
People if peace is dying who will answer our children
How I know you How I know you How I know you
Give us peace in our time
Bring us peace in our time

Zoom

The cameras' wide angle lens
Reflects in my wide eyed iris
Zooms out from my bed
Out above the city
Whose arteries pump with travelling cars
Zooms out miles into the vacuum
I still see me
A speck on the face of the Earth
In a tiny country – asleep
Night lights glimmer
Twinkling through a laser thin mist
I still see me
Hibernating on the dark side of a planet
Spinning on its axis
If I'm lucky
I may live to see it spin
Around its sun 100 times
Like a particle dances around the atom
Like the rings round Saturn
Like the patterns in nature
This white speck
A mere instant in infinite time
Zoom in again
I find a picture of an atom in my mind's eye
I ponder the big bang
I blink erasing it from my dream
We start again

Memories Of Childhood
Frank Curran
Retired Editor, Derry Journal

When I was invited to write an article on childhood memories, I was prompted to take a trip back to Westland Avenue, where I spent the first eleven years of my life.

As I walked up one side of the street and back down the opposite side, I was reminded of the words of the song – "Slowly I wander through scenes of my childhood, they bring back the memories of happy days gone by." How evocative, how true the words rang in my memory. Yes, those were happy years, when my generation was growing up in Westland Avenue.

Of course the street has changed. The families, the children of my generation have long been replaced by other families, other children, whose childhood years have been marred by the troubles in our society. Even the children today face pressures and dangers which never confronted us.

My family and relatives illustrate the changes time enforces. There were ourselves, my father, mother, sister Anna and myself. Next door my cousins, the McCarrolls, my aunt and uncle, sons Frank and Jim. And in number 37, my other cousins the Arthurs, my aunt and uncle, and their eight children, four boys, Frank, Bill, Gerard and Leo, four girls, Peg, Dolly, Anna, and Maeve. Of those eighteen people, only my sister and I survive. Again the words of the old song echo the inevitability of change. Talking of the children of his day, the singer says "Where are they now, some are dead, some are scattered, no more to their homes will those children return".

Westland Terrace was immediately below the Avenue. The boys of Avenue and Terrace played together, and there lived my first close friend, Michael Devine, who became a well-known architect in Derry. We went to school together and remained close until his death at a relatively early age ten years ago.

The Westland area was composed then of the Avenue and Terrace. Westland Street and the surrounding streets of the present were in the future. From Westland to Cable Street, Watt's field, later Meenan Park in memory of Corporation Alderman Paddy Meenan, provided rough and ready leisure facilities for the large number of children in the area. The days of local authorities actually providing amenities were also a vision of the future.

I vividly recall the first car to be owned by a Westland resident. It was the proud possession of my cousin, Frank Arthur, and it was a red Citroën, with running boards used to step into the vehicle. It was an object of wonder and envy to us boys.

We made our own fun. There was football in Meenan Park and the smaller field immediately opposite Westland Terrace, leading to the Bogside. We also raced with old car tyres, propelled by a piece of stick, starting in the Avenue, over the back lane dividing Avenue and Terrace, on to the terrace and up again to finish in the avenue. We played cowboys and Indians and marbles. Three small holes were gouged in the roadway (nowadays it would be called vandalism) and the object was to get the marbles in the holes by propelling them by use of thumb and first finger.

The arrival of the ice-cream man was an event which sent us scurrying home to ask for two pence for a wafer. They did a good business. I often wondered in later years how hygienic the ice-cream was; but that of course was none of our worry then, and nobody ever seemed to suffer any ill-effects.

Another familiar figure was 'Slabbery Mickey', who came around with his barrow, looking to exchange primitively-made windmills for jam jars. In our childish arrogance we called him uncomplimentary names, referring with childish cruelty to a physical disability from which he suffered.

The year 1932 stirs a golden memory – my first visit to see Derry City play at Brandywell. My father brought me and Derry beat Portadown. It was my first glimpse of the legendary Jimmy Kelly and Donald Shearer. On the match programme, produced by the inimitable Eddie 'Hawker' Lynch, Shearer was described as 'E D R Shearer'. That was because he was an amateur, whose initials were used to underline that fact. I asked my father what E D R stood for, and he said "energy, determination and resilience" which sounded better than Edgar Donald Reid. I had to look up a dictionary when I got home to find out what 'resilience' meant.

Going to St Columb's Hall to the pictures on the night before the summer school holidays ended was a pleasant ritual, clouded somewhat by the thought of embarking on another school year next day. Buck Jones, Ken Maynard, Johnny Weismuller, James Cagney were among the stars in those days.

Going to school we went across Meenan Park, into Stanley's Walk, up the Dark Lane, down Corporation Street, and down Bishop Street. We crawled unwillingly; but going home we raced to see who could be first. On really wet days we got the luxury of the two pence fare to go in luxury in what was known as the Lone Moor bus. It travelled down towards Brandywell, and across Hamilton Street to reach Bishop Street. There were about eight boys from Westland at the College, and on one occasion the bus was late. When we arrived for first class, our unanimous excuse was rejected by a teacher not renowned for generosity and we got four of the best from his strap. There were few civil rights available then for students.

Our English teacher was a stickler for spelling and punctuation. One day, exasperated by an essay which displayed ignorance of those two fundamentals (which we are told by academics is even today a disease among scholars) he told us "Punctuation does matter, I will tell you a story to illustrate". The story went – "A barber put up a notice outside his shop. It read: What do you think I give you a drink and shave you for nothing. A customer went in for a shave and afterwards asked for his drink. The barber said 'you owe me sixpence, but I don't give free drinks'. The customer said the notice outside said he gave a drink and a free shave. 'Not at all' said the barber. 'Come outside. That notice reads – What? Do you think I give you a drink and shave you for nothing?' Punctuation does matter!

Childhood Memories

Dana – Rosemary Scallon
Singer and Television Host

I fondly remember my childhood, where everything centred around my parents, family and music. We lived at 35 Greenwalk Creggan and I attended the Holy Child Primary school. There are three boys and three girls in our family and I was the fourth youngest. My father was a barber and my mother, like so many of the Derry women, worked in the shirt factory. Dad also played trumpet – he had his own band – and mum played piano. I remember the many musical nights when we would all sing and neighbours would come in and join us. Robert, my eldest brother, often rehearsed with his band in the kitchen and Eileen, my eldest sister, rehearsed with her band in the sitting room and as usual mum played piano and brothers Gerald and John and sister Susan and I sang along.

I always looked forward to our Derry Féis Columbcille. It was a great time for meeting with friends and it was marvellous to watch and listen to so many talented people. Susan, John, Gerald and I entered the singing and piano competitions – which was a great family tradition. I always remembered Prizewinners night – it was the event of the Derry Féis week and not to be missed. The Londonderry Féis also provided the opportunity for everyone to meet and compete again.

Summer holidays were spent on day trips to Buncrana or Susan and I staying with my Aunt Mary and Uncle John Minihan in Portrush. We would help in their harbour shop during the day and either sing at the Northern Counties Hotel or enjoy Barry's amusements in the evenings.

My Granny Sheerin and Great-aunt Mary Hassan were an unforgettable influence in my childhood and as I look back I can see how they both, together with my parents, were an irreplaceable source of great wisdom and inspiration. I enjoyed my childhood immensely and I would not have changed anything.

College-Boy
Seamus Deane
Author

My Aunt Sally, my mother's sister, was lame, beautiful, overworked and underpaid. I regularly ran errands for her. She gambled on the horses, had a fierce tongue, and worked part-time in Mary B's bar, just round the corner. There was always a running dispute about how much Sally was owed; every week she told me she was pounds short, she was never paid overtime even though it had been agreed she would be.

I was ten, had just started secondary school and had to wear a school blazer. I hated the way it made me stand out. People would roll their eyes and say, "O look at the wee college-boy."

On this particular day, Sally told me to go up and ask Mary B to give me her wages and a bottle of Holy Water. Then I was to go over the back lane and put two pounds each way on the favourites in the first races, the two o'clock at Sandown Park and the two-fifteen at Redcar.

I had to kneel up on a bar stool to get Mary B's attention. "C'mon back here" she said. "Dan, let him though."

Dan was my uncle. He eased me down off the high stool and made a great show of escorting me to the end of the bar past the line of men. They half-turned on their stools, smiling. He lifted a flap on the counter, put his hand back in behind the little half door, unbolted it, and let me through with a bow and sweep of his arm. "We must be on our toes, now. We have a college boy in our midst. Would you look at the badge on the blazer and the Latin on it."

Two of the men, who wore hats, doffed them in mock respect and held them across their chests. "Aw, sure we shouldn't be here at all, with all this learnin' about." "In here", commanded Mary B. I followed her into the back room, where two cats lazed on the sofa. Hummel figures stood on the mantelpiece, a porcelain dog barked soundlessly on a low table and a wonderful, curved salmon leaped on a vase about blue and yellow waters. She picked up a brown paper parcel and an envelope. Her cheeks were rouged, her hair was dyed, her skin was full of little patches of tight wrinkles that showed up her face-powder. "Now. How much do you have to put on the horses for Sally?" "Two pound double, to win." "Holy Jesus, that woman's out of her mind. Here. Take these two pounds and you bet one pound each way and you tell her I told you to do it. She has no sense, always putting all her eggs in one basket. I told her time and again; always keep something back. Always hold something in reserve. You remember that yourself." "Yes", I said, while thinking about the money she kept back from Sally. "But don't say I said it. And give her that wee parcel too when you get in. It's Holy Water."

I could feel that it was a smallish, square-shouldered bottle. It did occur to me that it was a strange place to get your Holy Water from, but then everybody had Holy Water in little porcelain finger-fonts in the hallway. You blessed yourself going in sometimes; always when coming out and you put a dab of it on your lips to keep your tongue clean and your words true.

She followed me out to the bar. The men were still smiling. I scooted round the corner, turned up the back lane and into the bookmaker's shed. It was almost two o'clock. I placed the bet, got the slip and then hung on in the gloomy shed to listen to the on-course radio commentary. The racing pages of newspapers were pinned along the walls and the results sheet hung down like a thick ribbon beside the betting counter. Sally's horse didn't even make a showing until the last furlong. Then it came through to win. I whooped and ran out, clutching the betting slip.

"One leg of the double up, Aunt Sally, Richards won the first." She beamed. "God bless you, you'll bring me the luck today. Stay here now and pray the next one makes it. What price did he come in at? "Och, I didn't wait..." Even as I spread my hands to say so, I felt their emptiness and realised I had left the bottle of Holy Water in the bookies. "What did Mary B give you?" she asked, her hand out. I fished out the envelope and gave it to her. She counted out the pound notes, looked at the betting slip. Her handsome blue eyes jumped at me. "Pound each way. Mary B told me to; told me to tell you she told me to..." "You gom; whose money is it? Who were you going the message for? Am I your aunt or amn't I? You took advice of a stranger! Didn't I say two pound straight? You've robbed me of a rise, listening to that old painted bag instead o' me. By Christ, she'll pay if this next horse wins. What are you going to college for if you can't run a simple message? God, I knew my sister had faults but I didn't think stupid children was one of them. Did Mary B give you nothing else, the sour, interfering bitch?" "O yes, she said for me to come back for the Holy Water." "The Holy Wa... why didn't you take it there and then?" "I dunno. Maybe she had to get it blessed." At that she laughed and limped across the room to sit down on the fireside chair. It always made me wince to see her twist as she did on her bad foot, especially as she was otherwise to handsome and soft-shaped, with her golden hair and pinkish skin. "Get it blessed. That's the best yet. The stingy bitch—you go back there this minute and tell her I'll take it as it is; damn a blessing it needs. What's she up to anyway?"

I was off before she had well finished and asked around the bookmaker's shed about the parcel. The men looked down at me and shrugged and went back to their newspapers and betting slips. The clerk told me to skedaddle; he had enough to do without looking for parcels. There was nothing for it; I had to go back to Mary B.

She was polishing the glasses behind the counter and laughing at something the customers were saying when I came in to the gleaming bar. It looked even larger, higher and more crowded than before. She leaned over, quizzical. I half-mounted the bar stool, slipping slightly as I whispered to her, conscious that the bar had gone quiet. "Sally says have you any more Holy Water." "More Holy...?" Everyone laughed. "Hi, Mary B, give us all a blessing with this Holy Water; sure it's as good as a church in here." She kept staring at me. "Come you inside here."

I went under the flap and followed her in. She faced me, hands on her hips. The lines at each side of her mouth were trembling like whiskers. "Alright. What did she say?" "She just wants more Holy Water." "What did she do with the holy bloody water I gave you?" "She... ah, blessed herself. That used it all up." "Is that a fact? Well, you go round there and tell her from me that if she wants to bless herself again, she'll have to pay good money for doing it; and you tell her when she pays money for it she'll think twice about blessing herself so fast. D'you hear me?" "Yes." She frowned a little. "Why did she take it so fast. How'd she do on the horses?" "They both won." "Holy Jesus. You're not serious. So that's it. What prices?" "Three to one..." She nodded. "And eight to one." I bit my lip. "Mother of God. The once I try to save her money, I lose her a wee fortune. Is she ragin'?" "Out of her mind. She was crying. And she cursed." "I'll bet you she did. She'll curse me for a month. How much did we lose her?" I liked the "we", but I had to pretend to compute. "It's fifty pounds, including the bet. Lucky it wasn't a treble." I offered. "Sweet Redeemer, a treble. It's a wonder she's not up here lookin' for my blood. What in the name of god can we do? C'mon. You're at college. Think of something."

I pursed my lips. "Well, for a start, if she didn't come up to work tonight or tomorrow night and lost no pay?", All the wrinkles flew up from her eyes and her mouth so that her face looked as though somebody had pulled it tight from behind. She was smiling. "That's it. Tell her she has the two nights off." I nodded but looked as unimpressed as I could. She took the hint. "Not enough, no? Tell you what. You sit here." She went off to the cupboard and rummaged around. The men inside were shouting. "Blessed Mary, another pint of Holy Water, when you're finished praying of course." They began to sing Benediction hymns in chorus. I took the Latin as a reference to me but I didn't say so.

> "O salutaris hostia,
> Qui caeli pandis hostium;
> Bella praemunt hostilia,
> Da robur fer auxilium."

Mary B got more and more flustered. She bent down, opened the bottom door of the cupboard and drew from it a large golden bottle. She wrapped it in a sheet of brown paper and then began fiddling in her purse. Her stockings were wrinkled, her dress was hitched up on one side and her hair had got spikier, although it was still stiff.

"Sweet Jesus, why couldn't I let the stupid bitch waste her own money? Now I have to pay her with my own. Teach me a bloody good lesson about tryin' to do people a good turn. Mind your own business Mary B from now on and let them all go to rack and ruin. Them drunks out there will get one sharp lesson in short measure this night, I can tell you that, them and their blasphemous hymns. Here you!" She swung round, gave me the brown paper parcel and two large white five pound notes. "You give her that, tell her she has two nights off, and that I'm sorry I interfered. That's the best I can do. Now, you go out this side door, down there, not through the bar."

Only one thing remained... to see the result of the two fifteen. I shot into the bookmaker's. The second horse had not even been placed. Perfect. Back to Sally. She was resting her lame leg on a pouffe near the fire and looking glum. I handed her the parcel. She gleeked at it and then held it to her in wonder. "Is that what Mary B gave you?" I nodded. "Your second horse lost." "Don't tell me. I know. I heard the result on the wireless. Where were you all this time?" "Up at the bookies and Mary B's how much would you have won, Aunt Sally? "Ah they were both odds on Maybe seven or eight pound. That would have been grand." "Well, here, don't tell Mary B that." I placed the two giant fivers in her lap. "Mary B? Ten pounds! and a full bottle of whiskey, Holy Water, I mean." She laughed and pulled me down on to her soft breasts and her wet lips stuck briefly on my neck. The strangest sensations ran over me, chasing after odours of her body, her hair, her skin, her clothes, her breath. I pulled away, almost frightened.

"Before you tell me anything, let me tell you one thing. You don't go to college for nothing and I take back what I said about my sister. So there. And you're getting five bob for yourself and the money for a fish supper before I go to work." "You're not going to work, not tonight, nor tomorrow night. Mary B told me to tell you. She'll look after the bar." "O for god's sake, get me a glass for this blessed Holy Water. What am I trying to hide from you? – this whiskey. Then sit here and tell me everything, every last item. Oh, I knew you'd bring me luck. Imagine. Getting a rise on the horses when you don't win on the horses. If I never know heaven again, I'll have known it this once anyway."

After that, it wasn't so bad being a college-boy.

"I Remember, I Remember, The House Where I Was Born"

Sister Anna Doherty
Community Leader

It was 120, Foyle Road, that lovely road which wound its way alongside the silvery waters of the Foyle river famed in song and story. Sandwiched between the road and the river, the great Northern Railway snaked southwards, its steam trains chugging away to Belfast and Dublin.

Many of the people who lived on the Foyle Road were employed in the GNR and some of the railway men lodged with the good people who lived there, kindly, friendly, generous people whose hearts like their hall doors were always open and welcoming. This was a tight-knit community ready to lend a helping hand to the old, the sick and the needy. I was happy to belong to such a fine neighbourhood.

Sadness often visited our street. This was in the days when children suffered from diphtheria, scarlatina and polio. TB was commonplace. Accidents at work also took their toll. I vividly remember when one of our neighbours, Willie Connor, a linesman on the railway, had a very serious accident, losing his leg and subsequently his life. The whole street was stunned by his untimely death. My own family was devastated, as he and his wife had taken my newly wed parents under their wing when they first came to Foyle Road. The kindly older couple had lost their youngest daughter a short time before. It seemed such a cruel blow of fate. That was my first brush with life's tragedy and I remember the grief to this day.

In those days there were two big shirt factories on the Foyle Road, the Star and Tillie and Hendersons. Workers came there from all parts of the city. As a child I enjoyed watching the crowds of women of all ages surging up and down the street to and from work, their chattering and singing and laughter filling the air with vitality. These women were the backbone of Derry. Many of them had to run their homes, manage the money and look after their families while holding down a job, as many women still do.

In later years, working in Shantallow, I was to meet some of them again, now retired and enjoying their hard earned leisure. It was good to sit and talk to them, reflecting on times past and recalling events they had long forgotten. These were skilled needle-women, second to none. In those days there were over six thousand people employed in shirt-making and Derry shirts were famous the world over. The women took great pride in the perfection and finish of their work. It is sad to see that professionalism and skill lost forever to profit-making.

The war years were very hard on our parents with rationing of food, fuel and clothes, a big problem. As children we just accepted our lives and got on with it. When the air-raid sirens wailed their warnings fear gripped our parents hearts. Some fled to the open fields at Braehead but we all squeezed into the cubbyhole under the stairs for shelter. Later in the war we sought safety in the purpose built air-raid shelters on the street with other families. At length our parents took us to Ardmore to live, unable to stand the strain.

A family from England came to stay in our house because Foyle Road was safer for them. This was common practice at the time and lasting bonds of friendship were formed between the evacuees and Irish families.

Foyle Road was in the Long Tower parish, a parish unrivalled in this city at the heart of which stands St Columba's Church. Its magnificent marble sanctuary, stained-glass windows and ancient walls have witnessed the celebration of the sacraments for centuries. The seasons of the years were marked by many festivals but in Long Tower the feast of Saint Columba, our patron saint, on June 9th, took pride of place. Every parishioner wore an oak-leaf and when the bands in the procession trumpeted the hymn

"St Columba, St Columba,
 Holy patron of our town,
 While thy children sing thy praises,
 From thy throne in heaven look down"

Our hearts swelled with pride.

The people of the Long Tower were the very salt of the earth it was "care in the community" perfected, for although there was poor housing, overcrowding, unemployment and low wages, their generous-hearted and unstinting support of one another saw them through hard times together. It was there I found the inspiration, energy and enthusiasm for the work which I had the privilege to be involved in, in later years.

School days were happy days for me full of seasonal games from skipping and hopscotch in the spring to sleighing and sliding in the winter. I went first to the Long Tower Girls, then to the Preparatory School in Artillery Street and finally to Thornhill.

The bigger girls took care of the little ones at school and while they were allowed to share in the games they were kept in their place by their elders. I can remember taking a wee girl by the hand to school. Her name was Alice and I looked on her as a little sister.

Ours was a mixed community on the Foyle Road. We had no need for a Community Relations Council. Our joys, our sorrows, our pain, our pleasures were shared. Children played together. Adults of all religious and none socialised together. We went to watch the twelfth of August celebrations, enjoying the glamour of the bands and the banners, while they came to the annual Long Tower Carnival. In our street I learnt tolerance and how to live in harmony with your neighbours, lessons that have stood me in good stead throughout my life.

I could write a book about my city, its music, its singers, its choirs, its concerts and pantomimes. I love its old walls, the beautiful Guildhall, our two fine Cathedrals, the old Convent in Pump Street, the lovely parks, the city centre so cruelly laid waste in the seventies, but thanks be to God, living and thriving once again.

These are my memories of Derry the town I love well, and its people that I love even more. I'm glad to be able to share them with you.

The Apple Of My Mother's Eye
Paddy Doherty
Chairman, Inner City Trust

The most vivid memory of my early childhood was the sight of dozens of women filling the kitchen, hallway and out into the street, on their knees, praying. My father was in the back yard, distraught, being consoled by a group of women. My mother was dying but the people of the Bogside made it very difficult to snatch a mother from her children.

I was transfixed by all the activity as I wandered unnoticed from the kitchen to the yard and into the street feeling abandoned and confused. This had happened before and the result was always another addition to the family making it more difficult to regain the relationship which I once had with my mother. But there were other women in my life who filled the gap. My cousin Rose-ann, Kathleen across the street, Jean who lived in the corner house and particularly the nun who was my teacher at the convent school. I could barely see her face behind the veil when at the age of four years old I joined her class but it was love at first sight.

My mother didn't die on that occasion and lived to the ripe old age of eighty four. My love affair with my teacher lasted a whole year and I believed that she was as committed to me as I was to her. I desperately wanted to remain in her class but she betrayed me. I remember the day quite well as she and the head nun sat reviewing the whole class. This one was to go to Miss Doherty's class, this one to Miss Durnin, this one to remain for another year with his present teacher. When my name was mentioned, without hesitation the love of my life said "Patrick to Miss Doherty". I was devastated.

My brother Hugh from an early age loved animals. A procession of canaries, turtles, rabbits, pigeons, Kerry Blue Terriers and greyhounds dominated his childhood years. However he had an incredible hatred of cats which continued into his adult life. He carried out a relentless vendetta against the species and never went to the assistance of any cat which was unfortunate enough to stray into the back yard domain of his favourite Kerry Blue. This hatred I believe stemmed from an incident of absolute horror initiated by one of these creatures. I still remember his cries of anguish when a cat stole into his pigeon loft. Pigeons scattered in terror, the cat leaped and pulled them to the ground as they struggled to survive the onslaught within the confines of the loft. My father raced to the scene but in his excitement couldn't immediately open the door. I stood mesmerised with shock. Eventually the door was opened and the cat escaped between my father's legs. With blood dripping from its mouth it scaled the back yard wall in a flash and disappeared.

Out of a total of fourteen birds only six remained alive, some bearing the marks made by the marauding cat. He nursed every injured bird back to health and mourned the loss of the dead ones for weeks.

Hugh must have been no more than six years old when he began to look after those children who came after him and as he grew older he washed dishes, scrubbed floors and when my mother was ill he would have done the shopping. He was the apple of my mother's eye and I didn't like it one bit.

Cut Knees And Coca Cola
Roma Downey
Actress

In spite of weekly ballet lessons with Miss Watson, I must have been a clumsy child for I have several faded scars on my knees to prove it. Tripping with my library books in Brooke Park, slipping on ice running down Beechwood Avenue, tumbling down the steps in the playground of the "wee nuns" school. Cut knees, plasters, tears and once even "stitches"!

The stitches impressed my friends and as I recall, earned me a day off school. I had the whole couch to myself, my choice of television viewing (probably "Scooby Doo" or "The Wacky Races") crisps and proper coca cola, you know the kind that liked to teach the world to sing and not a generic supermarket brand. Lots of tea and sympathy, love and attention, it almost paid to fall down! Yes, I can look at my fading scars and they bring me my whole childhood, which (at least until my mother died) were happy carefree days, as childhood should be and as I hope my own daughters will be.

But some children have been hurt and left with bigger scars that will never fade, emotional scars that bring with them the memory of abuse. I don't know why anyone would hurt a child but I know we must help put a stop to it. We are the grown-ups, it's our responsibility to do what we can. And maybe by our example, we can help them to heal and teach them to trust again.

Earhart's Aeroplane And The Children's League Of Pity

James Eaton
Lord Lieutenant of the City of Londonderry

I was born in 1927 at my grandparents' home, the Great James Street Manse in Crawford Square. My earliest recollections include being taken to see Miss Amelia Earhart's aeroplane in 1932. She was the first woman to make a solo flight across the Atlantic. She planned to fly from Newfoundland to Paris, but landed at Gallagher's farm on the Springfield Road. Also remembered was the arrival of General Balbo's twenty four seaplanes and the official opening of Craigavon Bridge by the Lord Mayor of London, with great pomp and ceremony, both in 1933.

I was brought up with two sisters and brother along the Limavady Road. I had a happy childhood and a lot of freedom. I was allowed to walk and later cycle unsupervised to other children's homes to play. Mother of course had to know where I was going. The roads were not so dangerous in those days. Cars were a comparative rarity, motor lorries and buses infrequent. The local bus service terminus was half a mile nearer the bridge. My father was a keen gardener. The bane of his life was the herds of cattle which on most days were driven twice along the Limavady Road. The cattle arrived at Waterside Station and were driven past our house in the morning to rest and graze. Back they came in the afternoon on their way to the nightly Glasgow boat. The front gates had to be kept closed at all times, not to keep us in, but the cattle out of the garden. Woe betide any of us who forgot to shut the gates. We regularly walked unaccompanied to Sunday School. An attraction of this walk was stopping to watch hundreds of soldiers coming out of All Saints Church at a quarter to eleven. They were then "fallen in" on Clooney Terrace with much shouting of orders and stamping of feet, stopping what little traffic there was. When everything was satisfactory they marched back to Ebrington Barracks. They even took their rifles to church!

Catherwoods ran the local bus service until 1935. There were three routes – Browning Drive to Pennyburn, Dale's Corner (bottom of Glendermott Road) to Rosemount, and Guildhall to Lone Moor Road. I attended Foyle College Preparatory Department on Lawrence Hill from the age of eight. I and almost all the Waterside Foyle boys and High School girls travelled by bus. I only remember one boy being brought by car – how we envied him. The bus fare was one old penny. A ferry ran from the bottom of Browning Drive to Harbour Square. The fare was a halfpenny. If I wanted extra pocket money and it was a dry day, I walked to and from the ferry morning and afternoon and spent the penny saved.

Father played golf every Saturday afternoon, so Mother took us by bus to visit her parents in Crawford Square. On Sunday afternoons Father took us all to visit our other granny at Altnagelvin. Grandfather Eaton had died before I was born. My grandmother was a founder member of the Derry NSPCC Branch which celebrated its centenary three years ago. In the thirties the Society had a junior fund raising branch – The Children's League of Pity. Two fund raising parties were held for members each year, a summer one at Mrs James Colhoun's home. Our collection cards and money were handed in on arrival and cards for the next year given out. The card, a drawing of an apple tree had twenty blank circles where the fruit would ripen. Each sixpence earned or begged allowed us to colour in a red apple. A winter fancy dress party was held in the Counties Cafe, Waterloo Place. The Duchess of Abercorn, the Society's President, would judge the fancy dress competition, with the prize winners' photographs appearing in the three local papers, each then published three times per week.

Life was fun and games for the few as unemployment and poverty were rife. The imposition of the Border had cut Derry off from its natural and historic trading hinterland. This coupled with a world wide depression had a devastating effect on the trade and prosperity of the city. My family, like all others, did not escape unscathed. Eaton's bakery lost 65% of it's customers in the summer of 1933. Bread had been added, with only forty eight hours notice given, to the list of goods which could no longer be imported into the then Irish Free State. Pay-offs inevitably followed. There were no redundancy payments in those days, indeed a holiday with pay – and then for only one week – did not become normal until about 1935. Now that both parts of the island are united by common membership of the European Union, trade flows freely again. Derry has again become the regional trading and shopping centre. What a different this had made – you would not recognise the "ould place"!

The outbreak of war initially had little effect on daily life as far as I was concerned. The 'Black Out' was a nuisance, the silencing of the shirt factory horns made it more difficult to tell the time. The docks became an interesting place to visit following the arrival of destroyers in the port in June 1940. This was to lead to the build-up of Derry as a major naval base. Many buildings were requisitioned including the two which housed Foyle College. The start of the September term saw Foyle sharing the Technical College. It was chaotic.

There was just not enough space to accommodate both schools. The Upper Foyle building on Academy Road, formerly used only to house boarders, was however quickly de-requisitioned. To the great relief of both schools Foyle moved to the 'Upper' building, and I believe remained there until the end of the war.

Derry's only air raid occurred at Easter 1941. A single plane intent on dropping mines in the river missed its target. The mines landed in the Messines Park area, luckily some landed away from the houses. Thirteen people died that night, a number of houses were destroyed and many more damaged. Next morning some of my friends and I, like vultures, cycled to the scene in search of souvenirs and to view the devastation. We of course were not allowed near the damaged houses, but did find in a nearby sandpit pieces of material and a length of silk-like rope. We were convinced they had formed part of a mine's parachute.

June saw the arrival of ostensibly civilian American construction workers. Most of them were 'Seabees' (Construction Battalion) and donned their uniforms immediately the United States entered the war. They had come to build new naval facilities at Lisahally, a hospital and camp. They were a colourful and exuberant addition to the local scene. They loved children and provided what seemed endless supplies of sweets, by then rationed, and oranges which otherwise were unobtainable. The construction of airfields and the build-up of naval facilities, coupled with an insatiable demand from the armed forces for shirts, all helped to diminish the scourge of unemployment. Despite shortages, the standard of living improved.

I went away to a boarding school in September 1941, my only clear recollections thereafter were of the first sight of the barrage balloons floating over "the town I love so well" on my return home for holidays.

In Sunshine Or In Shadow

Brian Ferran
Director, Northern Ireland Arts Council

I was the first child born to Barney, a telephone engineer, and his wife, Susie, on 19 October 1940. In that winter, when I was a few weeks old, the only bombs of the Second World War to fall on Derry so severely damaged our home in St Patrick's Terrace, Pennyburn, that it had to be abandoned. We moved temporarily to Strabane. Shortly after the war, we moved again to a new home at Argyle Terrace close to my maternal grandparents. By then, I had a brother, Michael, and a sister, Patricia. In time, four more children were born into our family: Anne, Paul, Deirdre and Desmond. A happy atmosphere prevailed in this period of optimism, with stability in the family and in the city. Money was scarce but access to street games and to the countryside was free and everyone appeared to pursue many and diverse interests including walking, cycling, swimming, fishing and many ball games.

Although it was a significant family event, I have no memory of the bomb which destroyed our uninsured home. I have, however, an early memory of the fire which destroyed Watts Distillery in William Street. Memory tells me that I was wrapped in a blanket and taken by my parents with other sightseers to get a hillside view from Rosemount. Nearly thirty years later when I had become a father of two children, my own family watched, in the darkness of a Mediterranean night, the glowing volcanic eruption of Mount Etna in Sicily and I remembered the flames and the heat of Watts Distillery. It is possible that I did not witness the Watts Distillery fire. The inferno may have happened before I was born and my images could well have been constructed from stories told long after the event by my aunts and uncles and cousins and their friends. It was an age of innocence in pre-television times when conversation was enjoyed and the language used much richer than is now common.

My memory of growing up in Derry fifty years ago is romanticised and enhanced by many factors, the most important of which is that I have had the good fortune to work all my life in the arts. Many plays, novels, short stories and much poetry, film, music, painting and sculpture address the subject of childhood and my understanding of these works is based on my early Derry experiences. They informed my first encounters with nature, from the sweet smell of honeysuckle to the bitter taste of wild sorrel. These small sensations contrasted with the marvels of nature like the great winter snowfall of 1947.

The heating pipes froze and the school closed for what felt like a full year. In that post war period, milk was supplied free in school to every child. It sat outside and in winter it was the first to freeze. That banked snow lasted for six weeks and St Eugene's Primary School in which I was what is now termed a 'stakeholder' became an Alpine cabin. We believed that Argyle Terrace had moved close to the ski slopes. The slope of Duncreggan Road was the piste on which to shine the metal runners of our heavy wooden sleigh. This was a gentle practice ride turning into Meadowbank Avenue and sliding gracefully down on to the Strand Road. Soon we graduated to the steeper gradient of the Rock Road and then to a high speed ride down Lawrence Hill. The destination was always the same and, when we got there, we just turned around and trailed our sleighs, on the end of a short rope, back to the top of the hill to slide back down again. The brightness of the snow made daylight last much longer and we were allowed to stay out late.

When we eventually returned home, we listened to reports of the big freeze on the BBC Home Service, at 6.00pm, and on 'Athlone', at 6.30pm. We learned of electricity being cut off in Mullingar and food supplies running short in homes in the Sperrin Mountains. We talked of our own Alaska, our Greenland, and our cocker spaniel became a husky! I cannot remember what we ate on those days but it was not cheese fondue. It was more likely to have been meat from Billy Healy's, fish from Micky Quigley's or pork from the long walk to Biggers stone in Foyle Street.

The wooded environs of Londonderry High School and the Magee College football pitches were an important playground – our very own tropical jungle. In October and November, the majestic chestnut trees yielded eating chestnuts and conkers which lasted until Christmas. Most fell in the wind and were collected eagerly each morning before school. Some were taken down by a short, stout stick, accurately directed at the fattest chestnut which held tenaciously. Others were brought down by climbing high into the tree and shaking its branches. Once, while on such an escapade, Gerry Mullan's weight was too great for a thin branch. It broke and he and the branch came crashing to the ground with a great thud! He broke his arm and his leg and was knocked unconscious when he hit the ground. Stephen Donaghy and I thought he was dead and ran shouting for help. The ambulance took him to the City and County Hospital. It was my first experience of terror and it stayed with me for a long time. Since then, I have never climbed a tree; nor have I felt a desire to do so. Gerry's plaster of paris gave him distinction in the neighbourhood and we, his peers, felt envious.

In time, our interests moved to other things, to the fields, the hills, the rivers, the lakes; to walks; to runs; to long cycles; to apples and pears of the local orchards; to swimming in the salt sea of Lough Swilly. These were summer pursuits and summers then were longer and hotter. I remember well the tar melting on the road and sticking to new hair on sun-tanned skin, to khaki shorts, to grey flannel trousers. The only known method of removing it was with melted butter. It possessed the same power as a dockin' leaf in calming the sting of a nettle.

I can only vaguely remember the hours when schoolwork and home exercises were undertaken at the kitchen table. I do remember the smell of fresh ink, transformed from dark gunpowder with water, the sound of squeaky, pastel-coloured chalk on the blackboard and the feel of cramming the names of rivers, lakes and rocks for the 'qualifying' examination. Keeping the nine times tables, the names of all the capital cities of the world and what a young seal is called in my head was a worry. I was fearful that the knowledge would escape before I could write it down on the wide-lined examination page. Rote memory carried high value and was put positively to the test in the catechism class. It was driven to the limit with "Introibo ad altare Dei. Ad Deum qui laetificat juventutem meam", but it stuck! Although I managed the Latin, my bell ringing was excessive and shortened my career as an altar boy.

Above all else, wheels were important. When the snow melted, the sleigh became a buggy guided by a string. With affluence came the second-hand bicycle. Attention to essential maintenance was obligatory and punctures were repaired with the speed of a Formula One pit team. In time, and as a reward for passing some examinations, my parents bought me a gleaming new bicycle. I felt that I had gained this reward under false pretences because I had no memory – nor had my friends – of eleven-plus stress. We entered it like a toboggan ride and it was not until years later that I realised the significance of this success and of the gleaming new bicycle.

Days were eventful and every year heralded a new and more exotic adventure. I remember well the opening day of the municipal swimming pool in William Street on or about the Watts Distillery site. This brought us a long way from damming the water of the little Glen River with stones and sods to create a swimming pool. It had no chlorine and was, no doubt, a health hazard but no one worried. Young people didn't appear to worry in those days.

Derry represented the magic of Hollywood in Ireland with its six cinemas: The Strand, The Rialto, The Palace, The City, St Columb's Hall and, for exclusive pictures, The Midland across the bridge in the Waterside. Programmes normally changed in midweek, except when a blockbuster was on show, so it was possible to see many movies and I did. Cinemas were closed on a Sunday but you could see a picture in the Fairview Football Clubhouse for three pence, or free if you entered by the lavatory window. Each cinema had different levels of comfort, different seat prices and attracted a different clientele. All Saturday matinées were crowded and boisterous. It must have been a nightmare for usherettes and (rarely) ushers to control. Boisterous behaviour was the order of the day.

My own brand of mischief was undertaken with accomplices. We spent the morning on the quays by the river with our equipment which comprised a large cardboard box, a short wooden stick, about fifty feet of string and a small bag of maize. The purpose of the equipment was to capture pigeons. This was done by placing the maize on the ground under the cardboard box which was propped up with a stick. The string was tied to the middle of the stick and, at a distance of fifty feet, we waited for birds to fly – or more frequently walk – into our trap. Success rates were poor by any standard but we did catch a few, because of their stupidity rather than our skill. Often it would take three or four hours to catch two or three birds and this in a city populated by pigeon fanciers, with well-bred ringed birds accustomed to people. Our captured birds then nestled either into our pockets or inside our jackets and off we went to the cinema to take our front stall seats. The pigeons 'played possum' and, at an appropriate time determined by the action on screen, we released the birds into the beam of the projector. Consternation followed! Then, in turn, my friend and I played possum.

I often wonder if this was my real world or just the world of my imagination. Whichever, it allowed me to grow at my own pace, in confidence and competence. I am in no doubt that the pace of life then was slower but had an eloquent rhythm and was without the desperate violence of recent decades.

I understand exactly what President Bill Clinton meant when he said on his visit to Derry in 1995: "I want more than anything for the young people of Ireland, wherever they live on the island, to be able to grow up and live out their dreams close to their roots in peace and honour and freedom and equality".

Memories Of Rosemount Boy's School
Peter Gallagher
Director – North West Institute of Further
and Higher Education

I was still only three years of age when I enrolled in the Rosemount Boys' School on 1 June 1943. It was a big help that I had four brothers – Liam, George, Raymond and Jack, at the school before me, although it wasn't much help to me when a certain irate teacher threw a wooden duster at my little head on the first day when I peeped through the glass of my brother Jack's classroom where I was told to go to wait till he took me home. Apparently this particular teacher didn't like wee brothers.

Looking back at it, going to Rosemount at three years of age was probably quite an undertaking. It was only through peering over the roll book of my own time that I realised that some of my classmates whom I might have considered 'tough nuts' might have been as much as two years older than I was – quite an advantage at that age. This may have helped me develop whatever political, diplomatic or negotiating skills I may have.

Times were not easy although the war years had brought extra employment and money to Derry. Nevertheless, I recall one family of boys who came barefoot from Sheriff's Mountain to the Rosemount School. My early years at school were punctuated by occasional nocturnal sorties dressed in my pyjamas into one of the two air-raid shelters in Epworth Street to await the "all-clear".

The war and especially the bomb in Pennyburn (which had killed 13 people and injured as many more) led to our being evacuated periodically to Muff where my father's sister Susan was the district nurse. My brother Jack made his first Communion there and whereas those of us who made our First Communion in the Cathedral got a Communion breakfast of tea and Sonny Fleming's buns up in the school, Jack had to settle for a plate of stew in Muff, courtesy of Hollybush School. Significantly, though, Jack was the only one of our family to become a priest – it just goes to show you how good stews are for you. Jack showed in another way in Muff that he had priesthood on his mind. In those years, sweets were nearly impossible to get but my aunt would occasionally get presents of white flat peppermint sweets, probably for delivering somebody's wean. Her son Willie who was aged between Jack and myself and who also became a priest was persuaded by Jack to play Holy

From left to right: Delcan O'Kelly, unidentified, Jim Campbell, unidentified, Charlie Anderson, Jim "Buddy" McDaid, John Harley, Jim McDonnell, unidentified, unidentified, Charlie Grant, unidentified, Dan Coyle, unidentified, John Hutchman, Peter Gallagher, Charlie Harkin, Joe McDaid.

Communion and he (Jack) would let him (Willie) be the priest and the white flat peppermint sweets would be the Holy Communion. I think Jack's ambition would have been to be at least a daily communicant. Sadly, my brother Jack passed away just a few months ago. I hope that Willie who pre-deceased him a few years ago will not have been waiting for him to settle an old score.

The war years brought other things as well, of course, like sailors from many countries with chewing gum, foul-smelling cigarettes and strange names many of which remain in Derry as a result of their possessors marrying local girls.

The end of the war brought me my first great street party in 1945. By that time, I had spent a year with Miss Rosena McVeigh (later Carrigan) and with the legendary Miss Mary Ann Coyle in the Babies and Senior Infants classes learning my first school song "O Do You Know The Muffin Man" and telling Mary Ann daily of impending visits home by my sister Marney who had gone to work in Stormont at the tender age of sixteen.

First class was next and our first male teacher, Mr Joe Campbell, but sadly Mr Campbell became terminally ill and we had a series of 'subs' for the year – among them, Miss Sheila McGuinness who drenched us with Holy Water during thunder and lightning storms and Mrs Molloy who threatened to burn our boots if we didn't keep our feet at peace. I have a memory of one teacher (who will be nameless) who when he started to slap, literally didn't know when to stop because the boys played 'keep the kettle boiling' with him i.e. when a boy got his dokes or whacks with the strap or cane, he went straight to the back of the long line of boys waiting for their dokes. The boys kept this never-ending line going till the poor man was physically exhausted. Clearly, the boys thought more of the crack than the whack.

Since life begins with conception we may consider the time we spend wriggling about in the womb as part of our childhood but when does childhood end? I am not sure whether I should have been pleased or angry when not many years ago one of my daughters asked me "Daddy, what are you going to be when you grow up?" I suppose I'll know when the time comes.

Of Bulls, Bilberries And Bygone Heroes

Roy Hamilton
Local Historian

Memory, it is often said, plays tricks and as time passes, the more opportunities there are for the memory to develop these. But, just as in any situation, there are two sides to every story... the good and the bad, so it is with memory. Now Human Nature being what it is, we tend only to remember the good. That said, it would be less than honest if I looked to memory and blamed it for tricking me into believing there were, in my childhood, bad times, because nothing could be further from the truth.

I grew up in Rosemount, in Lewis Street to be more precise. I was born in 1943 and grew up in an area which had, it seemed, to have everything necessary for a happy childhood. The Rosemount area was always known as "The Village" which in fact was an area bounded by Osborne Street, Creggan Road as far as Marlborough Hall opposite Rosemount Police Barracks, Warke's Lane which ran along beside the boundary wall of Brooke Park and then met Park Avenue beside the Rosemount Factory to join up with Osborne Street again. The streets which fell within "The Village" were Osborne Street, Artisan Street, Donegal Street, Cottage Row, Lewis Street, Rosemount Terrace and Warke's Lane.

As well as all that, right on our doorstep we had Brooke Park, a marvellous playground for football and all sorts of ball games. To all of us it was known as Brooke Park and it was only years later that I discovered, looking at the name displayed on the entrance gate beside Christ Church, the Church of Ireland church on Infirmary Road, that it was really Brooke's Park. The reason for this was that the money to build the park had been donated by the Brooke family whose estate had been on the Ardlough Road.

But it was not only Brooke Park that was our playground. The streets of "The Village" were a mixture of racing car tracks, (although truth to tell our "cars" were bicycle wheels without the tyres... hoops, which we guided with a piece of stick), they were cricket pitches with the stumps being chalked against the gable wall and where you needed a wet tennis ball to show when the stumps had been hit, otherwise the arguments between bowler and batsman would have gone on all day, and they were also prairies of the wild west over which we roamed looking for "baddies" and "goodies", depending on which side you ended up. For these escapades our trusted steeds were the self same hoops, but sometimes if some of the younger children wanted to join in, the only way we would allow them to take part was for them to have a rope passed around the back of their necks and under their arms with the two ends being held by us older ones so that they became our trusted steeds and ran in front of us, answering to instructions like "Whoa, Trigger" or "Hi Ho Silver". Our heroes and partners for travelling these trails were people like Roy Rogers, The Lone Ranger and Tonto, Gene Autrey, Lash Larue, Hopalong Cassidy and Tex Ritter.

Escapism was also realised every Saturday morning when I got my pocket money and sallied forth to the Rialto cinema to become an ABC Minor. On the way from Rosemount we stopped off at Woolworth's to buy a "Penny Dainty", a rectangular piece of McGowan's toffee, about two inches long by three quarters of an inch wide by half an inch thick. This delicacy was taken to the edge of the footpath, held in the palm of your hand and broken in two within its wrapping. The purpose of this was to have refreshment for each half of the performance in the Rialto. Threepence gained you entrance to the Minors and every Saturday I turned up to join the queue and eventually enter the fantasy world of "The Pictures". Here our heroes would be people like Flash Gordon, out to save the world from destruction from outer space, each week leaving you wondering if he was going to escape the evil clutches of his captor Ming and live to fight another day. There were also liberal helpings of cartoon characters like Bugs Bunny and Donald Duck, but to us, there were interruptions which only served to heighten the excitement of our hero's plight. It has to be said, though, that we weren't allowed to see the cartoons until the superintendent of the cinema, a Mr Hines I believe, came out on to the stage and informed us that the cartoons would not begin until we had picked up all our "sweetie papers" which, in our excitement we had discarded on to the floor. "Right boys and girls, pick up all your papers or there'll be no cartoons".

To strengthen our feeling of belonging we learned the anthem of the ABC Minors, a club which I understand flourished all over the United Kingdom, and so every Saturday we shouted our way through the song. "We are the boys and girls well known as, Minors of the ABC, And every Saturday we turn up to sing the songs we like and talk about the shows ..." and here memory plays one of those funny tricks because I can't recall any more.

But growing up in "The Village" was not all in the realms of fantasy. I can just remember when I was about three or four, coming back with my mother one day from playing in Brooke's Park. I was riding a tricycle and unknown to us a bull had escaped from a nearby field and had strayed into Lewis Street, down which it came as we approached the street from the other end. Our paths met at Paddy Sweeney's shop at the bottom of the street. My mother grabbed me and ran into the shop. The bull, determined to take out its anger on someone or something, lowered its head and put its horns under the handlebars of the trike, bouncing it off the gable wall of the end house. We watched from the comparative safety of the shop until we felt it was safe to come out and, on retrieving the trike, discovered that the handlebars were very badly twisted. They remained that way for as long as I had the tricycle.

Trouble, they say, never comes singly. Whilst recovering from whooping cough, I can remember being taken by my mother and father to visit some friends outside Moville. The friends lived on the hill outside the town, on the road to Kinnego Bay, and on the day of the visit I was proudly wearing a new light fawn coloured jacket. Three streams met at the top of the heather-clad hill, and it was well known in the area that a cure for whooping cough was to take the person suffering from the ailment to where the streams met and perform some ritual. I don't believe that I ever knew exactly what that ritual was, but I was carried on Mary Jane's (the lady of the house and friend of my parents) back up to the meeting of the waters and the ritual performed. That part of the story today has faded into significance. What has followed me down through the years is what happened on the way back to the farm. I apparently spied some bilberries among the heather and Mary Jane and I stopped to pick them. Some of them we ate, but some I wanted to take back with me and the only receptacles were the pockets of my brand new, light fawn coloured jacket. Bilberries are purple and light fawn is light fawn and never the two will form an alliance. For as long as I had that jacket, the stains remained in the pockets, and as if they weren't reminder enough of my misdemeanours, my mother never ever let me forget them. In later years when I thought about the incident, I remembered never ever being able to work out how Mary Jane had escaped from the incident without a blemish on her character, more than could be said about the jacket.

Today, reflecting on those carefree days of growing up in an atmosphere of love (with the possible exception of "The Tale of the Dreaded Bilberries"), the memories come flooding back. Days of Sunday School excursions, days spend riding the range in pursuit of "baddies", day trips to Donegal, long warm sunny days spent in Brooke's Park... good days, days filled with friends and friendships, days with not enough hours in them, days to be cherished for ever.

"Maggie Magee Makes A Good Cup Of Tea"

Ann Hasson
Actress

When I was born my family lived in Marlborough Road – a house with 2 bedrooms and at the time an outside bathroom. In a city rife with unemployment my father was lucky – he had a job. He worked as a credit collector for Hills. I remember my mother telling me that when my father got paid on a Friday night he would call at the shops on his way home to settle his weekly bills and by the time he reached the house there was usually nothing left over. Still we knew we were well off. There were families in Derry living in one room tenements with barely enough to eat. My mam who was a farmer's daughter from the West of Ireland, had trained as a drapers assistant and had worked all over Ireland before coming to Derry. She fell in love with Derry and she fell in love with my father. They got married in 1938. My father always tells of how when he was growing up he used to say three 'Hail Mary's' every day to get a good wife. It was the best investment he ever made! He had a wonderful wife for 53 years (my mam, God rest her, passed away in 1991), and we had a truly wonderful mother.

I was the fourth child in the family. An only girl, I had four brothers, three older and one younger than me. As children we all slept in the one bedroom. I loved being in the same bedroom as my brothers. We had great fun. When my father came home from work my mother had us all bathed – in our pyjamas ready for bed. All my father had to do was play with us – all sorts of games. The five of us would line up on top of the broken dressing table while he lifted up each one of us in turn throwing us up somersaulting in the air – the bed a trampoline – while he made up cheeky rhymes about the neighbours – "Mrs McKean is a silly wee bean", "Mr Kelly loves his jelly", "Mr McCann is a very big man", "Mrs Carlin is a darlin'", "Maggie Magee makes a good cup of tea", etc, etc. We thought he was absolutely hilarious! He thought he was absolutely hilarious! Then when we fell into bed hysterically laughing ourselves into a state of exhaustion – the moment of torture – da would hold high above each of us in turn a square of chocolate saying "who is the best daddy in the whole wide world?" – "You are daddy" we would chorus our eyes transfixed on the chocolate high above our heads – opening our mouths very wide like birds to catch the hard bit of chocolate that would come crashing down painfully hitting our tender little gums. Ouch! The pleasure was worth the pain. Then at last the moment we loved when my mother would come to say our prayers and kiss us good night. These are very happy memories. The same routine continued every night until one night as usual, chocolate held high, my da said "who's the best daddy in the whole wide world?" and a little voice said "Mr Canavan". The game was up! My da could barely suppress his laughter. He was outsmarted at last. But we still continued to play the game, partly for his sake, but mostly for the chocolate!

I was inconsolable when my parents moved me out of the boys room and I had to sleep in a camp bed in their room. However, when we moved to a new house and I was given my own very special room, I started to come to terms with this puzzling segregation. Still we continued to have a great sense of togetherness, even as we got older, and my da never lost his sense of playfulness. Often in the evening, after being out our separate ways, we would end up with all our different sets of friends packed into the kitchen listening to the Beatles and munching tea and toast. We would just be at the high point of the evening, when someone had told a particularly good joke and we would be splitting our sides with laughter, when the kitchen hatch would suddenly fly open, my da's face would jut out and he would shout "Rosary!". Chaos! People flew with their toast in all directions – back door, front door, side door, windows! Sometimes a poor unfortunate, who just couldn't get out through the window quick enough, got caught (much to my father's delight) and would be dragged into the room for the Rosary and the trimmings. My father was very ecumenical – Catholic or non-Catholic, you would still get stuck with the Rosary. It was yet another example of his very wicked sense of humour. In spite of this torment, our house continued to be very popular even though newcomers would always be warned by our friends to "WATCH THE HATCH!"

And then one day one of the brothers came home and announced he was engaged. An era had ended!

Happy Times

Laurence Hasson
Austin's of The Diamond

My da was a big man, a sheep farmer from the mountain of Mullahash in Feeney, and my mother was a small woman from the same town. They fell in love and eloped to Scotland where they got married. They came back to Derry where I was born in 1910. I had three sisters and a brother. I had a very happy childhood and went to school in Bridge Street and then to the Christian Brothers. I played football with the great Jimmy Kelly, a former international, and also in the street. I recall on one occasion I kicked the ball into a bread cart and out came all the bread and buns.

I looked forward to the summer holidays and we went out to my Aunt Mary's in Feeney for six weeks. It was great helping them with the turnips, cutting the corn and big spuds. We would go to the mountain to cut turf and my Aunt Mary brought us tea and scones for lunch.

We went to Feeney by Roberts bus. If the bus was full, we were put on the top with our feet dangling over – what a view! It was great when you were going around corners. The weather seemed to be always dry. Those were the days my Uncle Roddy always took me in the horse and cart to all the fairs, where he brought and sold sheep and cattle, and then into the pub for a drink over a sale – I got lemonade. The holidays finished all too quickly and then back home again.

Every Friday night was pay night – my da always gave me and my brother sixpence and I spent 4d for the pictures, 1d for a bar of chocolate, and 1d for two and a half Wild Woodbine fags. When cutting the fag in half the shopkeeper would squeeze it so much that you could hardly smoke it. Half a fag for Pathé News, one for the comedy, and one for part 4 and 5 of the big picture.

My da's hobby was shooting, so often he brought me out to Mullahash to shoot moorfowl. He carried me on his back, in his bare feet, and we would tramp for hours, then stop for something to eat. When I grew a bit older, about 15 years, he got me a gun from my uncle and taught me how to shoot. I remember shooting a hare and a moorhen, and I nearly shot myself on one occasion. I had walked into a green marshy bog, with the gun at the ready, after a moorhen and sunk almost 2 feet and the gun went off.

Those were very happy times.

"Peggy's Leg" And Rosemary Clooney
Maureen Hegarty
Soprano

I have lovely memories of my childhood. Some of my earliest memories are of trips to Moville every Sunday with my mother and young sister, Caroline. I loved Moville but hated the journey – I was always a bad traveller and still suffer from travel sickness. My parents were both from Moville so we had lots of cousins, uncles and aunts there. The smell of turf as we stepped off the bus – hmmm, I still love that smell. And the little bars of home-made rock, "peggy's leg", which we bought in a little shop in River Row round the corner from my granny's. Caroline and I were the two youngest of a family of eight children so we were always brought on these trips to Moville. I don't know if it was to keep my mother company or to keep us out of mischief, but it did not matter, it was a very big part of our childhood.

When I was 13 years old I was chosen to be a member of one of Ireland's most famous children's choirs, "The Little Gaelic Singers". We travelled to America and stayed for three and a half months, moving from east to west and back performing in concerts in great halls and colleges. We appeared on the national Ed Sullivan TV Show around St Patrick's Day and met Vic Damone, who was also singing on the show. He was a very big star and even though I was young I was impressed by the fact that he spent some time chatting with us. While we were in California we were taken to the CBS Recording Studios in Hollywood. I shall never forget the excitement riding on the bus to Hollywood with a police escort ahead of us. We waited for a short time outside the Studios, then out appeared Bing Crosby and Rosemary Clooney – this was the perfect dream come true – standing outside a film studio talking to two of the biggest stars ever to come out of Hollywood. We even sang for them "Eileen Aruin", a beautiful Gaelic love song. My autograph book is still one of my prize possessions.

It is while writing this that I realise what a great childhood I had. I lived all my life in Derry and had lots of opportunities to travel. I had great parents, brothers and sisters and a large extended family. Thank God for all of them.

From Donegal To Derry
Danea Herron
International Athlete

I am an ever-young mother of two living in Templegrove in Derry and have the distinction of competing in yet another senior track and field international this year. At thirty-eight years old, I am proving age is no barrier to competing at this level.

I was born in Dungloe in 1959 and lived for nine years in Glenties where my father, well known writer Frank Harvey, and mother, Agnes (well known in golf circles), had brought up their family of five girls. The family moved to Donegal Town in 1968 and it was there that I first acquired a taste for sports. Almost every youngster in the town had joined the St John Bosco Club and I was no exception. Two people who impressed and encouraged me at this were Michael Cooney and Tom Conaghan.

My first sporting love was soccer, followed by badminton. Track and field was not in my mind at this stage. I attended Gortnor Abbey in Mayo for a year but being a wee bit home sick I persuaded my parents to let me return to Donegal where I finished education at the local secondary school. The influence of Eamon Harvey and Deirdre McGrath opened my eyes to the skills of sport in general and I adapted very quickly to various sports competing in cross country, throwing javelin and competing on the school basketball and volleyball teams. I also gained qualification as a swimming instructor and took local children under my wing.

In 1979 I joined the staff of Bank of Ireland in Moville, a location where I took up water sports... sub aqua and water skiing. For a time, these took precedence over all else. Then I met Jim Herron, a Derry man, well known GAA player and athlete who also worked with the same bank in Ballybofey. Jim persuaded me to take up athletics and although I had little background in track and field, I soon made a big impression, not only on the opposition, but also on Jim. Jim and I married a few years later and we settled in Ballybofey. I competed for the local Finn Valley Club and within two years I had become Donegal's first female athlete to win All Ireland Senior Titles. These I gained in the heptathlon in both 1984 and 1985.

International competition followed. At Home Countries, International and European standard competition I always acquitted myself well. I have taken numerous titles over the years with Finn Valley, Foyle Valley and my current club Olympian. I have also won both the Donegal Sports Star Award, and since moving to Derry, the Derry Sports Star Award.

Amidst this success Jim and I have had two beautiful children who have no choice but to spend time on the track as dad coaches mum.

This year has been typical of success... one European Medal, five Irish Indoor Titles, three Irish Outdoor Titles, three British Sliver Medals and a Senior International Vest. Keeping down a full-time job, looking after a family and training several times a week would be a difficult task for any person but I enjoy it very much.

What of the future? The Veterans' World Championships in 1999 is the next big target and I know it will mean hard work, hard training and good competition to get there in peak condition. Retire? No chance!

Growing Up In The Glen
John Hume
MP and MEP

When I was growing up in Derry, there was a great sense of community and you weren't just from Derry, you were also from some district in Derry. I was from the Glen, a district on the outskirts of the city including Glenbrook Terrace, Glenview Avenue, Glenview Street, Hawthorn Terrace, Cedar Street, and added to it was what was known as the Scotch quarter – Glasgow Street, Glasgow Terrace, Argyle Street and Argyle Terrace. Other districts were Rosemount, the Brandywell, the Bogside and the Waterside. Creggan was just being built. From the Glen to the border was all green fields. So were Shantallow and Carnhill – indeed the Glen Road was the boundary of the city.

Each district also had its own football team, strengthening the sense of community. Rosemount and Glenview Swifts were two of the teams, and any game they played was a derby. Foyle Harps was the Brandywell team, and the Bogside had two teams – Wellington Rovers and Nelson Celtic. They played in competitions organised by the 'D & D' (Derry & District) in the Brandywell, and in Rock Park on the Glen Road organised by St Eugene's Boys' Club.

Most homes did not have television in those days and there was very little traffic on the street. Most of the people went down town on buses. In fact, there was only one car in my street – Glenbrook Terrace – that of Johnny Bradley, the taxi man. Streets were therefore our playgrounds. Football was often played with balls made of socks, and ropes made swings around lampposts. Hide-and-seek was also a common game. In the winter snow we sleighed on the streets.

Communication and neighbourliness were very strong. Everyone knew everyone. No-one could afford to buy all of the comics so most bought one – Beano, Dandy, Hotspur, Adventure, Wizard – and we swapped. There was a local shop in virtually every street. There were no supermarkets and the local shop wasn't just the place where we bought goods, it was a gossip centre as well. In our street McNutt's was the shop. In Glenview Avenue it was McLaughlin's, in Glenview Street it was McBride's, in Hawthorn Terrace it was Bonners's, and in Cedar Street it was Mick Kane's. Mick was an elderly man who was a great character. Finlay's was the local butcher's shop and Alec McLoughlin's was the fish and chip shop. The 'chip shop', as it was called, was a major source of food, particularly on Fridays. And indeed the street corner was the club where the men of the district met at night to discuss.

A stream, or a 'burn' as we called it, ran down the Glen Road at the bottom of our street, and beyond it were all green fields right out to the hills of Donegal. Nissen huts were built in Springtown during the second world war to house the American Navy. Derry was their European HQ and the baseball pitch was close by on the field that is now the Glenvale estate. We as children would go and watch them and learned to play baseball. In the summer we would build dams in the burn in order to go for a dip and swim.

In those days we had many 'characters' as well. The best known in our district – the Glen – was Jackie McClean, well known as 'Wabbits'. Nicknames were very common. 'Wabbits' was famous because he was a great hunter of rabbits and he called them "wabbits" – hence his nickname. Rabbits were very plentiful in those days in the fields and streams around the Glen. 'Wabbits' caught them and sold them as they were a popular food. His brother Brendan, or 'Brendie' as we called him, was someone of whom we were very proud, because he was a great footballer and played for Derry City.

We also had 'Tossy' Daly, another character, who delivered newspapers door to door. He spoke with a stammer and had a nerve in his arm, so very often he could not let go the knocker when he came to a door, and many people used to complain to him because of the noise. On one famous occasion in Hawthorn Terrace, Mrs Mowbray came out to complain to him and he said to her, with a stammer, "here's your paper and here's your knocker". The knocker had broken off in his hand.

Another great character was Maggie McCay who was a beggar. She said her prayers in the Cathedral at the top of her voice, and we all understood her and paid no attention. One day a stranger, a very posh lady, was kneeling beside her and Maggie was shouting her prayers as usual. The lady tapped her on the shoulder and said "excuse me madam, would you mind lowering your voice, you are distracting me". Maggie looked her up and down, looked at the altar and shouted at the top of her voice "as I was saying, Our Lady of Lourdes, before that hoor interrupted me...". Johnny 'Cutems' was another great street character who collected empty jam jars, and 'Hawker' Lynch who advertised in the Brandywell by carrying billboards at half-time and engaging in extremely funny banter with the crowds. There are no similar characters in Derry today because they have all passed the 11+! All the well known characters were clearly high intelligent people who in those days did not get the education that is available today.

The changes in Derry in the second half of this century are enormous, in housing alone. When I was a child Shantallow, Ballymagroarty, Carnhill, Irish

Street, Creggan and Gobnascale housing estates did not exist, and that clearly underlines the serious housing problem that existed. In many cases more than one family lived in the same house. My own family lived in one room in Southend Park in the Brandywell until I was four years old. That was common in those days. The men were mostly unemployed and women worked in the shirt factories. There were ten shirt factories on the West Bank alone, and women also did shirt work at night at home.

Our generation was also the first generation to get free public education. This started in 1947. Education is one of the main factors that has transformed our city. Had there been the same education in earlier times, all our famous characters, who were highly intelligent people, would have been university professors! Up until our generation went to St Columb's College, it had quite a small attendance by sons of businessmen and professionals. The sudden increase, because of the large number of working class children who passed the 11+, led to a large number of Nissen huts being built in the grounds in order to house the new pupils.

When the history of this century is being written, education will be seen as the main factor that transformed the community and indeed the city.

Snapshots

John Keanie
Town Clerk & Chief Executive, Derry City Council.

Recalling childhood memories has reached epidemic proportions in Ireland. Is our present so complex and our future so unpredictable that we need to resort to the comfort of the past? The past is static and unthreatening. It can be observed, sifted, analysed, even lied about, if there are no witnesses. We can manipulate our account of it to squeeze out sympathy, to explain away our faults and to excuse our actions.

It had never occurred to me to write about my childhood. Who would want to read about an ordinary boyhood in the Waterside? Red Doran had already done it in "The Story of a Derryman". Could our family's relative poorness be worked up into a tearjerker which turned out OK in the end because of the indomitability of the human spirit? No, Frank McCourt had captured this year's market share with "Angela's Ashes". Maybe I could weave a beautiful, dark, disturbing, poetic masterpiece which kept the reader wondering what was truth and what was fiction. Sorry, Seamus Deane just managed to pip me on that one with "Reading in the Dark".

Nevertheless, thinking back, recalling incidents and thoughts from long ago can be mildly habit-forming, even for the self professed sceptic. So what I'm going to give you is presented simply as a random selection of "snapshot" memories, some funny – at least to me – some sad, some slightly wistful but, hopefully, not mawkish. They are not meant to build to any great conclusion and are neither organised by theme nor arranged chronologically. Why these particular memories popped out is perhaps the only mystery of this piece. One thing which is common to them all is their clarity to me, their near presence as if they had happened yesterday. It makes me doubt if time can truly be a healer or even a distancer, and makes me selfishly glad that the horrors of abuse or neglect never visited me to brutalise me, to desensitise me or to be perpetuated like some curse handed down from generation to generation.

Second day at school. Four years old. It is January, snowing, as we walk up Glendermott Road and my skinny little legs are freezing in my short trousers. I don't want to go to school and I'm pretty forceful about it. My mother, in panic at this sudden insurgence, slaps my legs. So many years later she has never forgotten it, nor forgiven herself – beautiful piece of blackmail!

I'm five years old, at the corner of Bond's Place and Bond Street. It's 8.00pm and I'm sitting on the pavement with some friends. We've been trying out cursing, maybe for the first time, and along comes da to bring me in for bed. "You're a big shite!" I say – I suppose I got carried away by bravado. That was just before I got carried away to bed – I'm lucky it's not some of the other ma's and da's.

I've been sitting quietly on the old horsehair sofa at the front window in 6 Bond's Place. No-one else is in the room and it's starting to get dark. The sideboard is on the wall opposite me and there's a hole in the corner of the skirting board underneath it. This is where the little mice scurry out nervously for crumbs and whatever else is going. I like them. At least I prefer them to the silverfish in the damp cupboard under the stairs or the cockroaches which creep and stop, creep and stop, across the green linoleum. I wish the grown-ups wouldn't set those nasty traps. The noise, when they snap, scares me and the dark blood makes me sad.

Cousin Drew, Auntie Patsy and Uncle Walter are brilliant. I'm ten and Drew is seven and a half. We are standing in Patrick Street, about to get on the Swilly bus for Fahan. We've got a picnic basket and I've borrowed a pair of grey woollen swimming trunks. I hope they fit. The pavement is hot and I hope they've got plenty of drinks.

I'm thirteen now and Walter has just had a win on the horses. He's taking me with them for a week in Portrush – I told you they were brilliant!

I'm sitting in All Saints' Sunday School. I'm twelve and I've been thinking about this religion business. It's not for me. Twice on Sunday means two round trips from Mourne Drive to Clooney Terrace, no matter what the weather's like, and anyway, how can a King start a Church because he wants a divorce? When I'm fourteen and in long trousers I can make my announcement.

The rest of the class is laughing at me. I'm in the headmaster's class at Rossdowney Primary School and I've just been told off for betraying my ignorance. I thought a submarine cable was for tying up a submarine. I wish it was dinner time. They'll forget about it in the afternoon.

We've just got a Pye radio. It's red and cream Bakelite with a round dial with a pointer on it which points to words like Hilversum and Luxembourg. I could sit up all night with this, listening to the songs about school hops and dancing and girls. I'm going to get a guitar and play in a rock-'n'-roll band.

I left my granda to the Irish Street bus-stop and I'm walking home, looking at the half-crown he gave me. He seemed very sad and he told me to do well in my Junior exams tomorrow. Maybe his artificial leg was hurting him. That was Churchill's fault. He only ever swears if he mentions Churchill. He says he's an old bastard. He's not my full granda. That was James Wallace, who died in the First World War. That war took my other granda, Francis Keanie, too. Not many boys have had three grandas! My da says a lot of people who got a battlefield commission were shot. They only had a pistol and they had to be out of the trenches first to lead the men.

Granda's dead. Auntie Lena found him. He was sprawled across the bed. She says he must have felt ill and was trying to get into bed. Lena is hurting because he died on his own while she was at the factory. He had the artificial leg half off. I wonder did he think about Churchill.

It's October 1962 and I'm cycling home from games at Springtown. I've sneaked out early because I want to be at home if they drop the bomb. I wonder will I make it. I think three o'clock is the deadline. Kennedy is tough, but Khrushchev seemed mad enough to keep going. I wonder what it will feel like. I hope I get home.

I'm fourteen now and I've got the long trousers. The suit is new and I'm soaked walking up from All Saints. Ma, I've got something to tell you...

"Days Like This"
Carita Kerr
Former Mayoress

I woke very early that morning – long before the radio alarm. I lay in bed for a few minutes, and then I remembered – this was it – this was D-day, or should that be C-day!

Taking a shower was a bit of a pest – how on earth do you wash one side whilst keeping the other side dry? But that was the strict instruction from Altnagelvin and who was I to disobey them?

After overcoming that obstacle, I struggled into my clothes, drank a quick cup of tea and raced off to the hairdressers. She was amazed to find me on her doorstep when she arrived to open up.

Three quarters of an hour later, I returned home with every hair in place, on the motley, the paint and the powder as old Pagliacci put it, and I was ready.

The car arrived to collect us at 10.00am and we set off for City of Derry Airport, collecting the Chief Executive and his wife and the MP, MEP, and his wife on the way.

The airport was thronged with people by the time we arrived – the staff and their families had all been invited to be there on this special day. Upstairs in the VIP lounge food was laid out for the many important people gathered there, but no-one seemed to be hungry. We stood around and chatted in an aimless sort of way, whilst watching the American secret service men in their identical trench coats (the first time I saw them on the streets of Derry, I had mistaken them for Mormons!), talking up their sleeves to one another.

Eventually, the chief security man, Ed, told us that it was time to move downstairs and out onto the tarmac. As we stood waiting outside, a disembodied voice in Ed's earpiece said: "He's airbound. Over to you Ed". At that point, Ed turned a paler shade of green, I felt my legs turning to water, and the Mayor's heart leapt into his throat. But all three of us manfully recovered and gazed expectantly towards the sky.

A helicopter appeared and everybody got very excited and started waving their little flags. "He's not on that helicopter" Ed whispered in my ear. Another helicopter appeared – "He's not on that helicopter either" Ed again whispered in my shell-like. And a third time Ed whispered the same message.

By this time, the three helicopters had decanted an impressive number of

VIPs including a formidable looking lady guarding the box with THE BUTTON in it.

At last Ed said, "Here it is" and indeed, there it was – the helicopter we were all waiting for. The pilot stopped directly beside the Mayor and me, the red carpet was rolled out, the door opened and there stood the most powerful man in the world – the President of the United States. I could not believe it was actually happening, but in true Derry style I said to myself "Catch yourself on!" and the feeling passed away.

The President and Mrs Clinton descended from the helicopter and immediately came to the Mayor and me, they shook hands warmly and then to my amazement, both of them hugged me. What a moment! Will I ever forget it – I was just floating on air.

The President went over to the waiting crowd – the children were waving American flags and their mums and dads were smiling and laughing.

And then it was time to start the journey to the Guildhall. There were two Presidential limousines, and none of us knew which one the President was in. The Mayor's car was fourth in line – just about the middle of the cavalcade. The journey into Derry was so exciting – all the way from the airport, the roads were thronged with people cheering and waving flags and banners – it was a moving sight. When we arrived at the Guildhall, our driver was directed to the side, underneath a large canopy. The Mayor, the Chief Executive and his wife, the MEP, and his wife and me were ushered into the Guildhall but the Mayor's driver was told by the security men to stay in the car. "This is a sterile area and you have to stay with the car". (So the driver stayed and stayed and stayed, missing all the activity both inside and outside the Guildhall, including the chance of being presented to the President and receiving a memento of the visit from him. He was very disappointed about this, but I rescued the situation a couple of months later, when I returned from the White House with a specially signed photograph of the President for the Mayor's driver – so that was a happy ending).

Meanwhile inside the Guildhall, the President was again meeting all the people gathered there – some of them lucky enough to have their photograph taken with the President and the First Lady. But the main business of the day was waiting outside in Guildhall Square – the Chief Executive announced the names of the platform party, and after some introductions of the important people, the Mayor at last said "Ceád míle fáilte go Doire Colmcille – People of Derry, I give you the President of the United States, Mr Bill Clinton". Guildhall Square erupted with cheering and shouting – there were people laughing and crying with joy – so much happiness packed into Guildhall Square. A day I shall never forget – a day when the President of the United States came to our beautiful, historic city and we made our own bit of history.

A Wonderful Place

Geraldine McGrory
Former Miss Ireland

When I was a child I just knew that I lived in the most wonderful place in the whole world.

I had a close family who cherished and protected me; and many loyal friends whom I loved and trusted. There was music, dancing and laughter; and long filled summer days on Donegal beaches. Xmas was a magical time when Santa Claus never failed me.

I always felt safe in Derry, even during its darkest days. I considered myself privileged to have been born here.

As I grew older, I began to wonder if perhaps these boundaries of enthusiasm for my native city and its people might be diluted by my future experiences in the wider world.

I've been lucky to have had the opportunity to visit many countries and to meet people of different races and cultures.

These were great experiences, the memories of which I will always treasure; but wherever I went, the pleasure of being there could never outweigh the joy of coming home to Derry. I am fortunate to live in such a wonderful place.

A Place Of Which We Are Proud

Bishop James McGuinness
Bishop of Nottingham

I have very good memories of my early years as I grew up in the city of Derry where I was born. Life in those days was peaceful and there was a wonderful spirit of generosity and neighbourliness amongst the people there. In spite of the poverty they had to endure, they always remained strong in their faith, loyal to the Church and considerate and compassionate to each other as good neighbours.

Over the years I have continued to return to my city and I am saddened at all the unhappiness that has happened there, especially during the troubled years when many homes were shattered and when many family ties were broken, not least through unproved deaths.

It is sadder also to know that there has been a steady decline in the upholding of family values. Once these are eroded then it is inevitable that society as a whole will suffer. This has lead in many cases to the breakdown of home life when a lot of anxieties and problems burst into violence at times. In the midst of all this are the children. It is sad that for many of them their memories of life at home will not be so joyful as mine have been.

It is my prayer that good sense will prevail and that those values that God has laid down for our guidance will be noticed and observed by all so that Derry will always be a place of joy and uplift and a place of which we are proud.

'True And Trusty' – After Two Lads...
Gerard McChrystal
Concert Saxophonist

My musical career got off to a very inauspicious start at St Patrick's Pennyburn School. I was part of the mass recorder choir at school, performing classics such as 'London's Burning', when one afternoon we were assembled in the main hall where the music teacher gave us an aural test. It was designed to highlight any talent for music and instruments were allocated on the results achieved. I was desperate to play the clarinet so was pretty devastated to be told that I'd failed this so called fool-proof test.

My dad was a member of St Columb's TA Band, based in the lower reaches of St Columb's Hall, and he often took me along to hear rehearsals. The band used to rehearse next door to the boxing club, on Monday nights. Even then, at the tender age of 9, I found it ironic that guys struggled to create harmony and unison together in one room whilst next door they were solely intent on battering the gruel out of each other.

My dad was keen to get me started on an instrument but the only one going spare was a cornet. I nearly went spare myself, coping with only using three fingers to play the valves instead of the healthy nine I used to employ for the recorder.

I sat in for a few of the rehearsals, always arriving promptly at 8.30pm. At around 8.40pm most of the senior members arrived down from Badger's Pub to begin playing. I always found this funny because the TA in the band's title stood for 'Temperance Association'. In retrospect, I would challenge anyone to play 'Our Director', 'True and Trusty' and 'Hootenanny' in a row without needing a wee bit of the black stuff to relax the old embouchure.

Although I sat in with the trumpets, I found myself being constantly drawn to the sound of the clarinets. They seemed to dance above the rest of the band like demented nymphs in the high register and when they played in the low chalameau register they reminded me of the earthiness and stability of my grandfather, sitting in his chair overlooking the Brandywell.

After two weeks I gave up on the cornet – no more puffing of the cheeks, having the shape of a polo-mint engraved on my lips and the sweet aroma of Brasso emanating around my room. I just had to get a clarinet!

I can still remember vividly to this day the excitement of my first clarinet. It was late and I was in bed pretending to be asleep, having just survived another 'moon-walk'. (I shared bunk-beds with my sister Martina – I slept on the top one and would roll back the mattress exposing the wire base underneath. I would attempt to walk across 'the face of the moon' whilst underneath Martina would poke at my feet with her bony fingers until I fell down. This wasn't nearly as bad as the moment several seconds later when the mattress would come down on top of me, making me into a human sandwich, and leaving my face with a perfect grid etched on it.) My dad came home from the rehearsal, quite late again as usual. It was only when I joined the band that I realised that rehearsals went on for an hour but the following committee meeting often took over double that, being reminiscent of a bad day at the Commitments over the area of subs and who was in the lead in the late-payers stakes.

He produced a small, scruffy black case with two latches on it. I was a bit disturbed at first when he opened it to see that the clarinet was in five pieces. It reminded me of those puzzles they used to set contestants in the Krypton Factor and it was devoid of any instructions, just like one of those MFI hi-fi cabinets I would buy years later.

By the next afternoon the dulcet tones of 'London's Burning' on Gerard's new clarinet were reverberating along Fortwilliam Terrace. My mum later admitted that when I started she used to turn the stereo up loud, but as I improved with practice she gradually turned the knob the other way.

The very first piece I ever played was called 'True and Trusty' which, although it sounded like a bad bet at the Shantallow bookies, was actually a lively march. I had to play the second trumpet part because one of my colleagues had left the clarinet part under the Belfast Telegraph after his tea earlier that evening.

I suppose I can trace my ambitions to being a soloist to the night of my first rehearsal with St Columb's, because I soon realised that the first players had all the tunes, whilst underneath the second and third players supplied the rhythm and harmony along with the low brass. After an initial burst from the solo instruments, the boiler-house – i.e. me and my fellow second clarinet players – played a series of non-ending E's using the rhythm

whilst the lead players, having recovered from their earlier exertions, entered with the big tune. Dessie Quigg and the late, great Hughie Carlin played lead clarinets, and Hughie used to console me by saying that it was much harder to be a good second player than a lead, as well as being the backbone of the band.

Well, that was it as far as I was concerned, the last time that I'd heard the terms hard work and responsibility used in that context had been at Mass the previous Sunday when Fr O'Connell was talking about child-rearing!

My first gigs were in Clonmany and Carndonagh, where we escorted the local scout group to church. How innocent escorting people to and from church was in those days. As we marched along in sub-zero temperatures, with fingers resembling Mr Frosty's, I appreciated only having to play one or two notes because every other digit was completely frozen. Once again the TA in our title was compromised by the numerous hot toddies being consumed – for medicinal reasons of course!

It was also in St Columb's TA Band that I realised that I had the ability to play from memory. We were doing a summer fete at Gransha Hospital which was always a lot of fun. As usual there were several bands taking part and, due to the proximity of the groups, the air would often be filled with sonic collisions as our rendition of 'Our Director' would collide with the nearby pipe-band's version of 'Scotland the Brave'. I practised every day until I finally made first clarinet and this was my first outing as one of the 'made' men. One of the other lead players had forgotten his music, pulled rank and commandeered my music. I marched with the band, my lyre empty, but as the trumpets blared out the intro to 'Our Director', I could suddenly see the notes right in front of me. I'd practised the piece so much to become a solo player that my fingers were just playing the notes, as if on auto-pilot. Years later, I would hear James Galway say "Don't practice until you get it right – practice until you can't get it wrong".

Funnily enough, I sold my clarinets last year, having lost my musical heart to the saxophone when I was seventeen on hearing that amazing sax solo on Gerry Rafferty's 'Baker Street' by Raphael Ravenscroft. I now teach at the Royal Northern College of Music Manchester, where I was a student, between doing concerts and recordings around the world from Hawaii to Wellington.

The music world can be a very cynical and ruthless business these days and I really feel that I have survived and succeeded on my naïve love of music itself. This is something that I can easily trace back to my days in St Columb's, especially to Hughie Carlin and of course my very first teacher Dessie Quigg.

I got married last year to the concert pianist, Kathryn Page, and we live in High Wycombe, Bucks, with her daughter Alice. I recently bought my first house and adorning the walls of our music room is a framed copy of 'True and Trusty' and 'Our Director'. (Yes Dessie, I did get my music back!) And I have such fond memories of our conductor, Jim Canning, in his soft spoken voice calling the band to order, "Right lads, 'True and Trusty' after two...".

20-a-side On The Streets Of Creggan
John O'Neill
Former International Footballer

My earliest recollections seem to revolve around the year 1966. That was the year England won the World Cup and Everton came from two goals behind to beat Sheffield Wednesday 3-2 in the FA Cup Final. I think my interest in football must have started about then, as I would know most of the Cup winners after that year but almost none before.

I grew up in Creggan and have lots of fond memories of the streets and the people. Our major concern in those days was how to sneak into the neighbour's garden to retrieve our ball without being told off. Most of the time we played football in the street or in the field where St Peter's Secondary School now stands, the team sizes rising and falling depending on what time you were called in for your tea. I remember games when there may have been as many as 20 on each side.

I had a great childhood in Derry and when the time came for me to go to England it was a great wrench. For the first six months I would look in the bathroom mirror in the morning and wonder "What am I doing over here?" I always came home for about 8 weeks each summer and when my playing career finished I had no hesitation in coming home for good.

Rare Birds
Anita Robinson
Teacher and Broadcaster

Every year in Easter week, there may be spotted in great numbers, that breed indigenous to Derry City – the féis mother. Abandoning their spouses to a diet of chips and the housework, they congregate in large flocks at the Guildhall, where they spend a week twittering, squabbling and grooming their young.

As a species they are easily recognisable – generally having the well developed calf-muscles of the early Irish dancer, immensely strong kidneys and the iron digestion of a City Council refuse truck. Also stoicism of a high order to sit unfazed through seventy-eight infant renditions of "Baidin Elemi", with the critical certainty that their wane is the best.

The féis mother pays for one seat but occupies three. This is necessary since she carries her temporary nest-building materials with her at all times.

These consist of a capacious handbag containing throat lozenges, Junior Disprin, kaolin-and-morphine mixture, half a toilet-roll and three emergency pairs of split-new dazzling white ankle socks. Her even larger holdall is crammed to capacity with mousse, gel, lacquer, pins, clips, rollers (foam and spiked), tailcombs (steel and plastic), brushes (various), bobbles, toggles, ribbons, hairslides, a battery-operated hairdryer and a gas-powered hot-brush.

Over her other arm are draped two or three coats and cardigans, while from her index finger is suspended the zippered portable wardrobe-bag containing "the féis frock".

The féis frock used to be a relatively simple garment. Now it would take the eye out of you. Lined in satin, stiffened with buckram, it's a riot of quasi – Celtic motifs picked out in fluorescent thread and further embellished with little bits of mirror glass. Despite the exquisiteness of its artistry, it is always too short, giving rise to ribald remarks from the louts in the lower balcony when its wearer has passed the age of puberty.

The féis mother is generally accompanied by one or more small children whose enormous knobbly heads are swathed in pink nylon scarves. You see, féis children are not prepared for competition in the comfort of their own homes where every modern facility is available. Not at all – they are garbed, titivated and rehearsed in the main thoroughfare of the Guildhall known as "the corridor". In the corridor, we witness the wholesale destruction of the ozone layer. A palpable fog of hairspray hangs in the air. The aroma of cheese and onion crisps permeates the atmosphere. Every second adult inhales deeply and thankfully on a cigarette. Giggling clusters of teenagers are strenuously ignoring the fellows they will have "got off" with by the time the next competition's over. There is barely room to stand; the noise is deafening and little boys in mustard-yellow kilts are sliding merrily through the melee on the shiny parquet floor shuttling empty Coke cans as they go.

In the midst of this bedlam, the féis mother has set up her temporary nest. Every available nook and cranny is choked with children being tweaked and teased into perfection. God be with the days when it was all done with a pocket-comb and spit – though the serious féis mother "it was said", used a secret recipe of sugar and water to stiffen petticoats and hairstyles to a uniform rigidity. It was also said (with whatever truth) that Ursula Doherty won every competition on the strength of her totally symmetrical ringlets, which bounced like bedsprings in perfect unison as she danced.

For the twenty-second time the pianist breaks into the "Rakes of Mallow". On stage a tiny figure, arms clamped to the concrete folds of her féis frock, points a pre-pubescent toe. Under her chair, the féis mother's feet dance every step with her child.

I walk down the Guildhall stairs with the féis mother and her friend. "See thon adjudikkitter!" snorts the friend " – all he's tist's in he's mouth so it is! He's fer nathin! Our Sharon got two seconds and a first in Moville so she did. What about your Donna!" The féis mother shakes her head. The friend's mouth turns down – all sympathy. Then she rallies – "Ach sure it gets ye outta the house so it does". She turns to me. "Does your wee girl not do nothin'!"

Football And Cricket At Duncreggan Road

Claude Wilton
Retired Solicitor

My childhood was comfortable. I was born in the old houses in Eden Terrace and was the youngest of two children – my sister was four years older. I went to Foyle College then in Lawrence Hill and on the first day sat on my school bag containing a couple of bananas (my lunch). Some weeks later I hung my blazer, that was wet and all dirty after a fall, over a stove and burnt it. It was not an auspicious start to my school career.

The area where I spent my school years was well mixed in every sense of the word and unlike today I cannot recall any time of sectarianism though there was some poverty and many houses were overcrowded.

We had happy days playing football on a vacant piece of grassless ground near Richmond Hill (now full of garages) and my late father who was in the timber business supplied goal posts. Occasionally we played away fixtures at "Pats" field on the Foyle Road. Rugby was the only permitted game played in Foyle and although I preferred soccer I enjoyed the train journeys to various schools in the Province.

I could never understand why children were sent in almost all cases to segregated schools. Unfortunately this is still largely the case.

A lasting memory of these hard times in the twenties and thirties was watching people handing over a docket for free meal at Christmas – my mother was Mayoress for some years and we helped at this function. I think this was the first time I realised that the community was unfairly divided. It led to my later involvement in the Civil Rights Movement to try and ensure that each child received a fair opportunity in life.

I have fond memories of spending the summer holidays at my mother's farm and developed a great interest and love for animals that I still retain.

In the long summer nights it was pleasant to cycle to Fahan for a dip or swim or a bit of cricket or football in the old City of Derry Cricket Grounds at Duncreggan. Later we would watch and play in the Summer League.

Whilst I regret many aspects of my school days have faded in my memory, I am glad to say that I never encountered any bitterness. I hope and trust I have grown up to be broad-minded and tolerant if nothing else.

Mr Stephen Kelly
NSPCC
29a Strand Road
Derry

1 May, 1998

Dear Stephen,

Re: From Acorn To Oak: Memories Of Derry

On behalf of Mr Longs Supermarkets can I congratulate you on this venture and say how happy we are to be supporting this publication.

Mr Longs have a long tradition serving the local community and of supporting local causes such as the services that the NSPCC provide in this city. It is essential that organisations such as Mr Longs, who have a strong local base, contribute to help those helping the most needy in our society.

We are delighted to be given the opportunity to support the NSPCC through this book. Their tireless work piecing together the shattered lives of children and their families who have suffered from abuse has to be admired. It is vitally important that we as a community offer them as much support as we can in order to eradicate the abuse of children.

Once again, congratulations. We wish this publication and the NSPCC every possible success.

Yours sincerely,

Brian Long
Director

MR LONG GROCER

Woodburn
Strand Road
Greenhaw Road
Main Street, Eglinton
New Buildings
Melmont Road, Strabane

MR LONG WINESELLAR

Strand Road	Woodburn
New Buildings	Greenhaw Road
Main Street, Eglinton	Custom House Street

FAMILY DISCOUNT CLUB

YOU'LL WANT TO SPEND ALL DAY AT FOYLESIDE

OPENING HOURS:

MON-TUE	9AM-6PM.
WED-FRI	9AM-9PM.
SAT	9AM-7PM.
SUN	1PM-6PM.

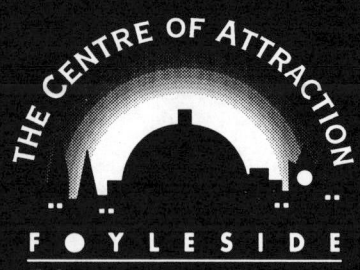

THE CENTRE OF ATTRACTION

FOYLESIDE *Shopping Centre*